1000+ Interesting Facts
For Interesting People

The Monster Guide

For those times when you don't know what to say or when you're being attacked by monsters!

By

Selene Triviani

1000+ Interesting Facts For Interesting People

Copyright © 2023 by Game Mechanics LLC

ISBN: 979-8-9883094-1-3

Disclaimer

The information presented herein represents the knowledge and views based on experiences, conversations and research done by the author up until the date of publication. While the author has made their best effort to make sure the information is accurate, they make no warranties with respect to the accuracy or completeness of the contents and specifically disclaim any implied warranties.

The author shall not be liable for any loss or profit or any commercial damages. This book is for entertainment purposes only.

Dedication

This book is dedicated to my students who would not back down because they loved the topic so much. If any success comes to this book, it is totally on them. I have done my best to gather the information I presented to them and have added more because there is so much more. Even with all that is in this book, it is just scratching the surface.

This book is also dedicated to all the crazy, fearless, funny, smart, and skilled readers who challenged me, in my head, every day while writing this book to get this information out there so that the people would know. It's important to everyone that the real word gets out. I have done my best. I hope it is worthy of you all.

Table of Contents

Introduction

Hey there fellow monster enthusiast! Welcome to my weird, wild, and wonderful world of creatures that go bump in the night. I've got a feeling you're the type of person who loves to drop some monstrous knowledge bombs on friends and family, and I'm here to help you do just that.

You see, I've spent a ton of time collecting stories, legends, and <cough> "facts" about all kinds of monsters. Sure, some of the details might be as stretchy as Mr. Fantastic's arms, but that's what makes it fun, right? I mean, who can keep track of all the ways to kill a vampire? Just in case though, I carry around a wooden stake, a garlic necklace, and some holy water. Better safe than sorry.

I've crafted this book for you with a little help from my computer buddies. They made some spooky digital artwork and helped me polish up the text. But don't worry, I didn't let them have all the fun - I put my heart and soul into this monster mash!

Now, you might notice that some of the images (like the Amityville house) aren't exactly, well, real. But hey, licensing the real deal would cost me an arm and a leg (and not the kind that zombies like to munch on). Besides, who needs total accuracy when we're dealing with creatures that probably (maybe?) don't exist?

So, dear reader, I hope you enjoy this monster-filled adventure as much as my friends and I have. And remember, if someone asks you about monsters, now you've got the facts to impress and amaze.

Happy monster hunting, and thanks for joining me on this wild ride!

Chapter 1
Ghosts and Hauntings
True Stories of Unexplained Phenomena

o **Home, Sweet Home:** A 2005 Gallup poll found that 37% of Americans believe in haunted houses. Does that mean they also believe in ghostly roommates that don't pay rent?

o **Unseen Undies:** Have you noticed how ghosts in movies are always wearing clothes? Does that mean there are ghost tailors working overtime in the afterlife?

o **Fearful Phantoms:** Surprisingly, many cultures believe that ghosts are more afraid of humans than we are of them. So, who's really doing the haunting here?

o **Hotel Room 873:** The Banff Springs Hotel in Canada has sealed off room 873 due to guest reports of horrifying paranormal activity. The hotel claims the room doesn't exist, but curious guests might find a missing spot in the room sequence...

o **Haunted eBay:** The "haunted" category on eBay is a booming marketplace. In 2000, a supposedly haunted cane sold for $65,000! That's one expensive walking stick.

- Pluckley Village: Dubbed the most haunted village in England, Pluckley is home to at least 12 reported ghosts. That's probably more than the local pub's regular crowd!

- Phantom Ships: The Flying Dutchman is a famous ghost ship doomed to sail the seas forever. Does it come with eternal seasickness, too?

- Helpful Haunts: The Bell Witch haunting in the early 19th century is one of the few recorded instances where a ghost helped a human - by offering farming advice! Talk about agricultural assistance from the other side.

- Ghostly Railways: The ghost station 'St. Mary's', part of the London Underground, closed in 1934 but reports persist of eerie noises and spectral figures. Do they still need to mind the gap?

- Presidential Hauntings: The White House has its fair share of ghost sightings, including Abraham Lincoln. It's good to know some politicians stick around to clean up their mess.

- Pet Ghosts: Some people have reported seeing the ghosts of their pets. It must be nice to have a ghost that fetches itself.

- Ghost Phones: Phantom phone calls are part of many haunting accounts, with strange voices and messages from the beyond. Does the afterlife have a good reception?

- Mummy's Curse: The infamous curse of Tutankhamun's tomb is well-known, but did you know it's considered a form of haunting? Still, it's quite the step up from a haunted house!

- Haunted Castles: Edinburgh Castle in Scotland is said to be one of the most haunted places in Europe. This includes a phantom piper, a headless drummer, and even the ghost of a dog!

- Running from Ghosts: In Eastern cultures, it's believed that if you're being chased by a ghost, you should run in a zigzag pattern as ghosts can only move in straight lines. Or maybe they're just really bad at geometry.

- Hitchhiking Ghosts: One popular haunting trope is the phantom hitchhiker, who vanishes after being picked up. At least they're low on emissions?

- Ghostly Vocab: The word "Poltergeist" is German for "noisy ghost". So next time you hear strange noises, it might just be a spirit who's had too much coffee.

- First Contact: Séances rose to popularity in the 19th century as a way to communicate with the dead. Who knew the afterlife could be just a
- Spectral Smells: Some people have reported experiencing specific smells before a ghostly apparition, like perfume or cigar smoke. Ghosts, just like us, seem to appreciate a good scent.
- Ectoplasm Excitement: The concept of ectoplasm, a physical substance produced by spirits, was popular during the Spiritualist period of the 19th and early 20th centuries. Think of it as ghostly goo... perhaps the afterlife should invest in some Kleenex?
- Roll Call for Ghosts: Ghosts are reported to be more active at night. Perhaps the afterlife operates on a different timezone, or maybe they're just not morning people.

Chapter 2
Witchcraft
Separating Fact from Fiction

- The word "witch" comes from the Old English wicce, meaning "wise woman." However, over the centuries, the term's meaning has dramatically changed - talk about an identity crisis!

- In the Middle Ages, owning a black cat could get you accused of witchcraft. These days, it might get you a ton of likes on a cute cat Instagram post. Times change!

- The infamous Salem Witch Trials of 1692 resulted in the execution of 20 people, but not a single accused person was burned at the stake - that's a myth popularized by Hollywood!

- Did you know there's a Witchcraft Act in England? Enacted in 1542, it made witchcraft a crime punishable by death. Thankfully, the act was repealed in 1735, but maybe avoid stirring a cauldron in public, just in case.

- Witches are not just female. In fact, men accused of witchcraft were often called warlocks, wizards, or even sorcerers. Talk about gender equality!

- Love potions and magic spells aren't just for Hogwarts. Some cultures believe in the power of witchcraft to influence love, health, and prosperity. Ever considered witchcraft as a career move?

- The iconic image of a witch riding a broomstick has unusual origins. It's thought to stem from a pagan fertility ritual. And you thought it was just a convenient mode of transport!

- In the 16th and 17th centuries, people used "witch bottles" filled with hair, nails, and urine to protect against witches' evil spells. Talk about a nasty cocktail!

- Some believe that witches hold their sabbats on Walpurgis Night (April 30th) and Halloween (October 31st). It's like having two witchy birthdays a year!

- During the European witch hunts, "witch prickers" were employed to find the devil's mark on accused witches. Ouch! A worse job than a dentist, for sure.

- "Cunning folk" were community healers and diviners in England who used folk magic for helpful purposes. Not all witchcraft was considered evil, apparently!

- Iceland takes its witch history seriously. The Museum of Icelandic Sorcery & Witchcraft houses many artifacts, including a pair of necropants (pants made from a man's skin). Creepy!

- Despite witch trials being a thing of the past, belief in witchcraft persists today. In fact, Wicca, a modern pagan witchcraft religion, has been officially recognized in the U.S. since 1986.

- The Malleus Maleficarum, published in 1487, was basically a "how-to" manual for identifying, interrogating, and prosecuting witches. Talk about a niche market!

- There's a town in Norway named Vardø where the Steilneset Memorial commemorates the trial and execution of 91 people for witchcraft in the 17th century.

- According to folklore, witches could transform into hares. So next time you see a bunny, you might be witnessing a witch's day off!

- The last person convicted under Britain's 1735 Witchcraft Act was Helen Duncan in 1944. And you thought the witch hunts ended in the 1600s!

- In the Wizard of Oz, Dorothy's nemesis, the Wicked Witch of the West, is famously melted by water. But don't worry, real-life witches can shower just fine!

- Witches' familiars, often portrayed as cats, dogs, or toads, were thought to be evil spirits in disguise, helping witches in their nefarious deeds. Today, they would probably have their own YouTube channels!

- The "witch's hat" has a disputed origin. Some believe it derives from the peaked hats Jewish people were forced to wear in the Middle Ages, while others argue it's based on the high-crowned, wide-brimmed style of the Welsh hat. Whichever the case, it's an iconic look!

Chapter 3

Vampires

The Legends and Lore Behind These Bloodthirsty Creatures

- The word "vampire" was not introduced in English until the early 18th century. Before that, these night-loving bloodsuckers were referred to by various names, including "blood drinker" and "undead."

- Despite what pop culture would have you believe, traditional vampires cannot transform into bats. This myth likely originates from the vampire bat, a real creature native to the Americas.

- Garlic as a vampire deterrent? It's a thing! In folklore, it's believed that vampires have an aversion to garlic. Remember to stock up on garlic bread for your next vampire movie marathon!

- The legend of the vampire was heavily influenced by real medical conditions. For instance, the symptoms of the rare genetic disorder porphyria - sensitivity to sunlight and gums receding from the teeth - eerily mirror those of vampirism.

- "Vlad the Impaler," a.k.a Vlad III, Prince of Wallachia, is often considered the real-life inspiration for Dracula. With a nickname like "the Impaler," you can imagine he wasn't the friendliest guy.

- The iconic fanged vampire image can be traced back to F. W. Murnau's 1922 film Nosferatu. Now, those pointy teeth are a staple of any vampire Halloween costume!

- The New England vampire panic in the 19th century saw corpses being exhumed and their hearts burned to prevent the dead from preying on the living. Sounds like the plot of a gripping horror novel, doesn't it?

- In Slavic folklore, vampires were said to have a left-handed shadow and could be spotted due to their lack of a reflection. Imagine the inconvenience at the hairdressers!

- Highgate Cemetery in London is known for a supposed vampire sighting in the 1970s, igniting a media frenzy and a vampire hunt. No actual vampires were found, much to the disappointment of local goths.

- Folklore suggests various methods of destroying a vampire, from a stake through the heart to decapitation. Remember, vampires are mythical, so please, no staking!

- According to the Gypsy (Romani) lore, to prevent a vampire from rising from the grave, you must place a steel needle in their heart. Talk about a harsh wake-up call!

- Mercy Brown, a girl who died in 19th-century Rhode Island, was thought to be a vampire when her body didn't decompose as expected. In reality, the cold weather had preserved her corpse.

- The Vampire Moth, a real creature in Japan, was named for its blood-sucking habits. However, unlike their mythical counterparts, these moths don't have an aversion to daylight.

- In the 18th century, Europe experienced a vampire craze, leading to mass hysteria and even public vampire stakings. No word on whether garlic sales also went through the roof.

- The Chupacabra, a creature from American folklore, is often described as a type of vampire due to its blood-sucking habits. The main difference? Chupacabras are said to prefer livestock, not humans.

- According to some folklore, vampires could be distracted by scattering poppy seeds or grains. They'd be compelled to count every single one, proving that even vampires can have OCD tendencies!

- Bela Lugosi, famed for his 1931 role as Count Dracula, was buried in his full Dracula costume - cape included. Talk about commitment to a role!

- Some vampires in folklore are said to be able to transform into wolves, not just bats. It seems Team Jacob and Team Edward from Twilight could have more in common than we thought!

- In the folklore of the Philippines, the Manananggal is a vampire-like creature that detaches its upper body from its lower body to fly around and prey on pregnant women. Yikes!

- Before the charismatic and sophisticated portrayal of vampires in popular media, these creatures were often depicted as bloated and of dark countenance - a far cry from the suave vampires in Twilight or Interview with the Vampire!

Chapter 4
Werewolves
The History and Mythology of These Shape-Shifting Beasts

- The fear of werewolves, or lycanthropy, was taken so seriously in Europe during the Middle Ages that people were actually put on trial and executed for suspected werewolf activity. It makes the Salem witch trials look like a garden party!

- Silver bullets as a method to kill werewolves made its first appearance in popular fiction, not folklore. Looks like werewolves had a lucky break until writers decided to give them a metal allergy!

- Clinical lycanthropy is a recognized psychiatric syndrome in which a person believes they're transforming into a wolf or another animal. Not to be confused with a strong desire to join a furry convention.

- In Greek mythology, King Lycaon was turned into a wolf by Zeus as punishment for serving him a dish made from the king's own son. Talk about an extreme version of "you are what you eat!"

- The oldest known reference to a werewolf story comes from "The Epic of Gilgamesh," where Gilgamesh refuses the advances of a woman who turned her previous lover into a wolf.

- In many folklore tales, werewolves are created when a human is bitten by another werewolf. Other stories suggest that you could become a werewolf simply by drinking rainwater from the footprint of a werewolf. So remember, hydration is important, but choose your water source wisely!

- The Beast of Gévaudan was a man-eating creature, said to be a wolf-like animal, that terrorized the former province of Gévaudan in the Margeride Mountains in south-central France between 1764 and 1767. Over 100 victims fell prey to the beast, giving it a terrifying place in the annals of werewolf lore.

- Werewolves have a significant role in the myths and legends of the Native American peoples, especially among the Ojibwe and the Cree. They believed that humans could transform into animals or other people, and vice versa.

- The full moon connection was a later addition to werewolf lore. Earlier tales simply had the transformation occur at will or via a magic salve or cloak.

- In Europe during the werewolf panic, people would wear belts made of wolfskin to protect themselves from lycanthropy. The irony seems to have been lost on them!

- Some historians believe that the werewolf hysteria was partly due to the effects of ergot poisoning from a fungus that infected rye crops. Apparently, hallucinations can make you see all sorts of things, including your neighbor turning into a giant canine.

- The town of Werewolf Springs in Tennessee was named after a local legend about a beast that was half-dog, half-wolf. As of my knowledge cutoff in 2021, no real werewolves have been spotted there.

- In 1589, a German man named Peter Stumpp was executed for allegedly being a werewolf. His nickname? The Werewolf of Bedburg.

- The legend of the Rougarou is a French tale of a human changing into a wolf, akin to a werewolf. In Louisiana, this legend became intertwined with local culture and is used to inspire fear in children who misbehave.

- In Slavic mythology, a person could turn into a werewolf by wearing a belt made of wolf skin, or if they were cursed or bitten by another werewolf. Talk about a bite worse than a bark!

- "An American Werewolf in London" (1981) is one of the most famous werewolf movies and was celebrated for its groundbreaking makeup and special effects. It even won the inaugural Academy Award for Best Makeup.

- Contrary to popular belief, werewolves and vampires weren't always enemies in folklore. That rivalry was largely popularized by modern media.

- J.K. Rowling's character Remus Lupin in the Harry Potter series is a werewolf, with his name referencing the legends of Romulus and Remus and Lupin derived from 'lupus', the Latin word for wolf. Talk about hiding in plain sight!

- In the "Twilight" series, the werewolves are actually shape-shifters, and their transformation is not dependent on the moon. Not your traditional werewolf, but hey, innovation is key!

- In Medieval Europe, it was believed that werewolves turned into wolves only under a full moon. This association has endured in popular culture, although early folklore stories didn't make this connection. So, the next full moon, think twice before planning a picnic at night!

Chapter 5
Demons and Possession
The Scary Truth About Evil Spirits

○ The study of demons and belief in demonic possession dates back thousands of years and is found in many religions worldwide, from Christianity to Hinduism. Academic rigor, meet supernatural study!

○ In Christian demonology, the hierarchy of Hell is cataloged extensively, with different ranks and types of demons. It's a devil of an organizational chart!

○ The most famous case of alleged demonic possession is probably that of "Roland Doe," a pseudonym given to the boy who inspired the 1971 novel and the 1973 film "The Exorcist." His real identity has been kept secret for obvious reasons — it's hard to get a job when your references say you're devilishly difficult to work with.

○ Have you ever heard of the demon named Valak? If you're a fan of "The Conjuring" movie series, you certainly have. Valak is represented as a monstrous nun in the movies, but traditional demonology describes this marquis of hell quite differently, often as a small boy with angel wings riding on a two-headed dragon. Talk about a makeover!

○ According to lore, King Solomon used a magical ring known as the "Seal of Solomon" to command demons to construct the first Temple of Jerusalem. It was like a biblical version of a construction crew!

- The Codex Gigas, also known as the "Devil's Bible," is the largest medieval manuscript in the world. It's said to contain a number of religious and historical documents, but its most striking feature is a large illustration of the devil. Not quite a coffee table book, unless you want to make a statement!

- Believe it or not, there is a patron saint for those who believe they are possessed by demons. Saint Dymphna is often invoked for those believed to be suffering from spiritual afflictions and mental illness.

- Paimon, a demonic entity mentioned in multiple demonic lexicons, received quite the fame boost when it was featured as a key character in the film "Hereditary." Paimon, we're ready for your close-up!

- Some cultures used to believe that sneezing was a sign of demonic possession. This was one of the reasons why the phrase "Bless you" came into existence. Makes allergies seem a bit more sinister, doesn't it?

- The tradition of exorcism, the practice of evicting demons or other spiritual entities from a person or place, has been practiced by many religions including Christianity, Buddhism, Hinduism, and Islam.

- The Lesser Key of Solomon, a popular book in demonology, lists 72 different demons along with their abilities, ranks, and the rituals to summon them. It's like a demonic phone directory!

- The infamous demon Pazuzu, from Assyrian and Babylonian mythology, was the demon that supposedly possessed Regan MacNeil in "The Exorcist."

- In many traditions, a possessed person is said to demonstrate certain distinct symptoms such as drastic changes in voice, supernatural strength, and speaking languages they've never learned. Spooky language lessons, anyone?

- Many demons in folklore are fallen angels, as per Christian tradition. They were cast out of heaven for rebelling against God, which just goes to show that office politics can get really out of hand.

- According to some Christian beliefs, the Antichrist will be the ultimate embodiment of demonic possession – a human fully possessed and controlled by Satan himself.

- Zozo is a demonic entity believed to communicate with people through Ouija boards. Pro tip: if you see the planchette moving to Z-O-Z-O, maybe take a break from the game!

o The Winchester Mystery House in San Jose, California, was built by Sarah Winchester, who believed she was haunted by the spirits of those killed by Winchester rifles. She thought that continuously building the house would appease these spirits. Now that's a housing market boom!

o The Bible, in the book of Mark, references Jesus casting a legion of demons out of a man and into a herd of pigs, which then ran into a lake and drowned. Talk about hogging all the attention!

o Anneliese Michel, a German woman, underwent 67 exorcisms during the last year of her life. Her story inspired the movie "The Exorcism of Emily Rose." It's safe to say that Anneliese probably wasn't a fan of pea soup.

o In several cultures, amulets, talismans, and tattoos are used to protect individuals against malicious spirits or demonic possessions. Forget fashion accessories, these are survival accessories!

Chapter 6
Ghosts Around the World
Haunted Places and Spooky Tales from Across the Globe

- The Tower of London is said to be one of the most haunted places in the UK, with numerous ghosts including that of Anne Boleyn, who was beheaded there in 1536. Seems like she really lost her head over that place!

- Aokigahara Forest, also known as the "Sea of Trees," at the base of Mount Fuji in Japan, is considered one of the most haunted places in the world due to the high number of suicides that occur there. It's even said to be home to yūrei, spirits of the deceased in Japanese folklore.

- "La Llorona," or "The Weeping Woman," is a famous ghost story in Latin American folklore. It tells of a woman who drowns her children in a river and is doomed to wander the earth, crying and looking for them. A real tear-jerker of a tale!

- The Great Wall of China is not only famous for its impressive size but also for its ghost stories. Many people claim to have seen ghostly apparitions and heard mysterious sounds while visiting. Even in the afterlife, it seems you can't escape tourist attractions!

- In Iceland, elves and hidden people, also known as huldufólk, are believed to live in rocks and hills. Disturbing these places can bring bad luck, and some construction projects have even been altered or abandoned to avoid their homes. Now that's environmental consciousness!

- Ancient Egyptians believed that the ka, or life force, left the body at the point of death but remained nearby. Tombs were stocked with food, drink, and personal belongings for the ka to use. Talk about a fully stocked afterlife!

- The Aboriginal people of Australia believe in spirit creatures that roamed the Earth, creating life and shaping the land, a period referred to as Dreamtime.

- In the Amazon rainforest, the indigenous Yanomami people believe in the yoshi, a malevolent spirit that can cause illness or death. They believe that yoshi are particularly attracted to blood and bodily waste, so maintaining cleanliness is a serious matter.

- In Malaysia, the pontianak is a vengeful spirit of a woman who died during childbirth. She's said to locate her victims by sniffing out hanging laundry, so maybe rethink airing your dirty laundry!

- Raynham Hall in Norfolk, England, is famous for the "Brown Lady," a ghost who reportedly haunts the grand staircase. Her most famous sighting was captured in a photograph published in Country Life magazine in 1936. Even ghosts can't resist a good photo op!

- The Island of the Dolls (La Isla de las Muñecas) in Mexico is a well-known haunted spot. The island is full of dolls that the former caretaker hung up to appease the spirit of a girl who died nearby. It's as creepy as it sounds.

- Poveglia Island in Italy is known as one of the most haunted places in the world due to its grim history as a plague quarantine station and mental asylum. Visitors are currently not allowed – probably for the best.

- The Catacombs of Paris, France, hold the remains of more than six million people and are said to be haunted by muffled voices and ghostly apparitions. It seems overcrowding can be a problem in the afterlife too!

- In Scottish folklore, the Blue Men of the Minch are said to dwell in the straits between the mainland and the Hebrides. They are known to cause storms and shipwrecks but will spare sailors who can out-rhyme them. Brush up on your poetry before your sea voyage!

- In Filipino folklore, the manananggal is a self-segmenting creature with a taste for human flesh and blood. During the day, it appears as a beautiful woman; by night, it separates its upper torso from its lower body and sprouts wings to fly in search of its next meal. It's a truly disarming tale!

- In South Africa, the tokoloshe is a small, mischievous creature believed to cause trouble for people while they sleep. If you wake up with inexplicable bruises or scratches, a tokoloshe might be to blame. Who needs alarm clocks when you've got one of these?

- The "Flying Dutchman" is a legendary ghost ship said to never be able to make port, doomed to sail the oceans forever. It is most associated with the Cape of Good Hope in South Africa. Sea you later!

- In Thailand, the Phi Tai Hong is the ghost of a person who died suddenly or violently. It is considered dangerous and vengeful, proving that some spirits just can't let go!

- Ireland's Loftus Hall is believed to be haunted by the devil himself and a young woman named Anne Tottenham. The story goes that the devil visited the house, disguised as a charming man, and won Anne's heart before vanishing suddenly. Some say Anne still waits for her lover's return.

- The ghost lights of Marfa, Texas, have been baffling people since the 19th century. These glowing orbs appear in the desert at night, and while there are many scientific theories, some believe they're the spirits of Spanish conquistadors searching for their lost treasure. Guess it's not all tumbleweeds and cowboys in Texas!

Chapter 7
Psychic Powers
The Strange Abilities of the Mind

- Edgar Cayce, also known as the "Sleeping Prophet," was an American clairvoyant who reportedly answered questions on subjects as varied as healing, reincarnation, wars, and future events while in a sleep-like trance. He'd probably do well on a trivia night!

- Uri Geller gained fame in the 1970s with his purported psychic abilities, including his trademark skill of bending spoons seemingly with his mind. Who needs a dishwasher when you can just unbend your cutlery?

- The Stargate Project was a real U.S. Army unit established in 1978 to investigate the potential for psychic phenomena in military applications, particularly "remote viewing": the ability to psychically "see" events, sites, or information from a great distance. Sounds like the perfect job if you're not a fan of commuting!

- The concept of psychokinesis, or the ability to move or manipulate objects with the mind, is a staple of comic book and science fiction narratives. However, despite numerous claims and demonstrations since the rise of spiritualism in the mid-19th century, no scientific research has conclusively supported its existence. That doesn't stop it from being a popular party trick, though!

o Jeane Dixon was one of the best-known American psychics of the 20th century, due to her syndicated newspaper astrology column and a series of popular biographies. She famously predicted the assassination of President Kennedy. Not exactly the cheeriest forecast!

o Nostradamus, a 16th-century French apothecary, is arguably the most famous psychic in history. His prophecies have been translated and reinterpreted in many languages due to their cryptic, poetic style. A poet and a psychic, what a combo!

o The term "clairvoyance," meaning "clear seeing," was introduced by French spiritualist Allan Kardec and refers to the ability to perceive things or events in the future or beyond normal sensory contact. It's like having a crystal ball without the ball!

o The Global Consciousness Project, originating at Princeton University, has been collecting data for decades in an attempt to identify the potential existence of a global psychic connection that could respond to major world events. It's like the world's biggest group chat!

o Psychometry, or "token-object reading," is the claimed psychic ability to glean information about an object or a person associated with it, simply by touching the object. Imagine what you could learn just by holding a library book!

o Many people report having precognitive dreams, in which they see events before they happen. Scientists suggest these may be the result of our brains processing information and making educated guesses about the future. Or maybe we're all just a little bit psychic.

o The concept of "Indigo Children" emerged in the 1970s, referring to children who are believed to possess special, unusual, and sometimes supernatural traits or abilities. It's like the X-Men, but with fewer mutants and more tantrums.

o A 2006 National Science Foundation report noted that 60% of American college students reported having had a psychic experience. However, skeptics suggest these can be explained by cognitive biases, coincidence, or misperceptions.

o The Society for Psychical Research was founded in London in 1882 to investigate paranormal phenomena. The "Ghost Club," also based in the UK, was formed even earlier, in 1862. Ghost hunting is an old pastime, indeed!

- The term "remote viewing" was coined in the 1970s by physicists Russell Targ and Harold Puthoff while working at the Stanford Research Institute. They used the term to differentiate their protocols from the less structured approach used in clairvoyance.

- Scrying, a practice dating back millennia, is a form of looking into a suitable medium in the hope of detecting significant messages or visions. The most common media used are reflective, translucent, or luminescent substances such as crystals, stones, or glass. Need a hobby? Try becoming a seer!

- In many indigenous cultures, shamans are said to possess psychic abilities, using their powers to heal the sick, communicate with the spirits, and guide their communities.

- Eileen Garrett was an Irish medium and parapsychologist who claimed to channel various spirits, including that of the deceased flight crew of the British R101 airship, which crashed in France in 1930. Talk about an in-flight service!

- Sylvia Browne was a high-profile American psychic and medium who made regular appearances on television and radio, including on The Montel Williams Show and Larry King Live. She authored many books on spirituality and offered private psychic readings. She saw success in her future and, voila!

- Leonora Piper, a famous American medium in the late 19th and early 20th century, was investigated by psychologist William James, who described her as one "white crow" — the one case that proved that all crows weren't black, in other words, not all mediums were frauds.

- Dowsing or divining rods have been used for centuries, often to locate water, minerals, or lost objects. Despite being widely considered pseudoscience, they remain popular in certain contexts — especially if you've lost your car keys!

Chapter 8
UFOs and Aliens
Investigating Reports of Extraterrestrial Life

- The term UFO, which stands for Unidentified Flying Object, was coined by the U.S. Air Force in 1953. It replaced the earlier term, "flying saucer," which came about after a misunderstanding in an interview with a witness to a UFO sighting. It's a bird, it's a plane, it's...unidentified!

- The Roswell incident of 1947, where a local rancher discovered unidentifiable debris in his sheep pasture, is arguably the most famous UFO case in history. The military maintains it was a crashed weather balloon, but that hasn't stopped the speculation. Weather balloon or alien Frisbee match gone wrong?

- In 1952, Washington, D.C. had a series of UFO sightings. Jets were scrambled, but pilots could not catch whatever was causing the radar blips. The incident led to the creation of the Robertson Panel by the CIA in 1953. Politics and aliens - it's a bigger circus than we thought!

- The Arecibo message is a 1974 interstellar radio message carrying basic information about humanity and Earth, sent to globular star cluster M13. The message will reach its destination in about 25,000 years. Better late than never?

o Crop circles, which first gained media attention in the 1970s, have often been attributed to extraterrestrial beings. However, many have been confirmed as human-made, often as part of a prank or for artistic expression. Aliens: they're just intergalactic Banksys!

o In 1980, near the Twin Bases of RAF Bentwaters and RAF Woodbridge, several sightings of unexplained lights and the alleged landing of an extraterrestrial spacecraft came to be known as "Rendlesham Forest incident." Now that's what you call a camp-out!

o The SETI Institute (Search for Extraterrestrial Intelligence) uses large radio and optical telescopes to search for signals from advanced civilizations. So far, E.T. has been pretty quiet.

o "Ancient astronaut" theories propose that aliens visited Earth in the distant past and may have influenced human culture and evolution. Erich von Däniken's book "Chariots of the Gods?" is a famous example. So, the pyramids might have been alien DIY projects?

o The "Wow!" signal was a strong, narrowband radio signal received by Ohio State University's Big Ear radio telescope in 1977. The signal's origins remain a mystery, leading some to speculate it might have been a transmission from extraterrestrial intelligence. Wow, indeed!

o The Phoenix Lights were a series of widely-sighted unidentified flying objects observed in the skies over Arizona, Nevada, and Mexico's Sonora state on March 13, 1997. Thousands of people reported the phenomenon, causing a media frenzy. The aliens just wanted to join in on Spring Break!

o In 2017, the U.S. Department of Defense confirmed the existence of the Advanced Aviation Threat Identification Program, a secretive program to investigate UFO sightings. X-Files, anyone?

o The Drake Equation, proposed by astrophysicist Frank Drake in 1961, attempts to estimate the number of extraterrestrial civilizations in our galaxy with which we might come into contact. Sadly, it doesn't help with estimating the chances of alien abduction.

o The Fermi Paradox highlights the apparent contradiction between high estimates of the probability of the existence of extraterrestrial civilizations and the lack of evidence for, or contact with, such civilizations. Maybe the aliens just aren't that into us?

o Betty and Barney Hill were an American couple who claimed they were abducted by extraterrestrials in a rural portion of New Hampshire in 1961.

This was the first widely-publicized claim of alien abduction. Talk about an unexpected road trip!

o The "grey" alien is the most common depiction of an extraterrestrial being in pop culture, often portrayed as a small humanoid with a large, bulbous head and big, black eyes. They've become the Hollywood A-listers of the alien world!

o Crop circles in Wiltshire, UK have drawn speculations of extraterrestrial communication since the 1970s. This area is considered the world's epicenter of crop circle activity. Who knew aliens were such aspiring landscape artists?

o In 2020, the Pentagon declassified three videos showing unidentified aerial phenomena. The videos had been leaked years earlier, causing a sensation among UFO enthusiasts. If only the aliens could have helped with better video quality!

o The idea of ancient astronauts and extraterrestrial influence on ancient cultures includes the hypothesis that the Moai statues of Easter Island were created (or influenced) by aliens. Who needs a crane when you've got interstellar friends?

o Some UFO enthusiasts claim the "black knight satellite," an object orbiting Earth, is of extraterrestrial origin. Skeptics and scientists, however, believe it's likely debris from a previous mission. One person's space junk is another's treasure, right?

o Area 51, a highly classified remote detachment of Edwards Air Force Base in Nevada, has been the center of numerous UFO sightings and conspiracy theories. Its intense secrecy is a perfect ingredient for speculation. What happens in Area 51 stays in Area 51!

Chapter 9
The Bermuda Triangle
Strange Disappearances and Mysterious Happenings

o The Bermuda Triangle, also known as the Devil's Triangle, is a loosely defined region in the western part of the North Atlantic Ocean where numerous aircraft and ships have disappeared under mysterious circumstances. Never has a geometry lesson been so intimidating!

o The boundaries of the Bermuda Triangle are generally believed to stretch from Miami, Florida to the island of Bermuda and down to San Juan, Puerto Rico. Next time you're drawing triangles, be careful!

o While the Bermuda Triangle has become part of popular culture, it's not recognized as an official region by the US Board on Geographic Names. This is the geographical equivalent of "it's complicated."

o One of the most famous disappearances in the Bermuda Triangle is that of Flight 19, a group of five US Navy torpedo bombers that vanished during a training flight in December 1945. That's one tough training day.

o The Bermuda Triangle gained fame as a mysterious region after journalist Vincent Gaddis coined the term in a 1964 magazine article. Talk about a branding success!

- Various explanations for Bermuda Triangle disappearances include magnetic anomalies, methane hydrates, rogue waves, or even extraterrestrial activity. All are equally reassuring.

- The 1977 film "Close Encounters of the Third Kind" features the Bermuda Triangle. In the film, Flight 19 returns, complete with its crew, aboard a giant spaceship. No news on whether they had in-flight meals.

- The Bermuda Triangle is one of the most heavily traveled shipping lanes in the world, with ships crossing through it daily for ports in the Americas, Europe, and the Caribbean islands. It's the ocean's version of a busy intersection.

- The idea of the Bermuda Triangle as a dangerous place comes largely from writers who have embellished or fabricated reports to enhance its mystery. Not exactly the best travel endorsement.

- The SS Marine Sulphur Queen, a tanker carrying molten sulphur, is one of the most famous ships to disappear in the Bermuda Triangle. It vanished without a trace in 1963. A hot case indeed.

- Some speculations suggest that the lost city of Atlantis is located beneath the Bermuda Triangle. How's that for an underwater neighborhood?

- Bermuda Triangle incidents have been reported since the time of Christopher Columbus, who reported seeing strange lights and experiencing compass malfunctions. Old school mysteries!

- The USS Cyclops, with 309 crew onboard, is one of the biggest losses in the Bermuda Triangle. The ship vanished without a trace in 1918. The sea isn't always the best confidante.

- Methane gas hydrates, which exist on the ocean floor, have been proposed as a possible cause of disappearances. The theory suggests that gas eruptions could reduce the density of the water, causing ships to sink. Remember, kids, always check for gas leaks!

- Bruce Gernon's "Electronic Fog" theory, based on his own experience, suggests that a time-warping tunnel within the Bermuda Triangle could cause the disappearances. Makes one ponder, "To fog or not to fog?"

- The Bermuda Triangle is sometimes linked with the Dragon's Triangle, a similarly mythical area off the coast of Japan. Because, why should the Atlantic have all the fun?

- Some skeptics argue that the Bermuda Triangle doesn't see any more disappearances than any other comparable region of the ocean. It's just that its PR team is unbeatable.

- The Bermuda Triangle was prominently featured in bestselling author Clive Cussler's novel "Serpent." Makes for an "enthralling" read!

- The Bermuda Triangle lore has also made its way into video games, like the 1982 Atari 2600 game "Bermuda Triangle: Saving the Coral." Game on, explorers!

- Despite its ominous reputation, cruise ships are commonly seen sailing through the Bermuda Triangle, and flights frequently fly over it. Next time, try a "haunted triangle" vacation package!

Chapter 10
Cryptozoology
Discovering Creatures That May or May Not Exist

- Cryptozoology, derived from the Greek words for "hidden," "animal," and "knowledge," is a pseudoscience involving the search for animals whose existence hasn't been proven. Think of it as a wild game of hide and seek!

- The study of cryptozoology often includes the search for legendary creatures like Bigfoot, the Loch Ness Monster, and El Chupacabra. It's not your typical zoo.

- The field of cryptozoology isn't recognized as a branch of zoology or a discipline of science. It's like the rebel child of scientific studies.

- Cryptozoologists often refer to these unverified creatures as cryptids. They're elusive, they're enigmatic, they're...cryptids!

- The coelacanth, a prehistoric fish thought to be extinct but found alive in the 20th century, is often cited by cryptozoologists as evidence that cryptids can indeed be real. The coelacanth - the cryptid that got away!

- Famous cryptozoologist Bernard Heuvelmans is often called the "Father of Cryptozoology." He wrote the book "On the Track of Unknown Animals" in 1955. Talk about a unique career choice!

o Cryptozoology combines aspects of zoology, folklore, history, and mythology. It's like a salad bar of academic disciplines.

o The International Cryptozoology Museum in Portland, Maine, houses exhibits about cryptids and mysterious animals. It's the place to be for all cryptid enthusiasts!

o While most scientists are skeptical of cryptozoology, it does have a following in popular culture, with numerous TV shows, movies, and books exploring cryptid sightings and hunts. It's a cryptid world out there!

o Some cryptids, like the Yeti and Bigfoot, are believed to be large, ape-like creatures. Meanwhile, others, like Scotland's Nessie, are said to resemble ancient marine reptiles. Diversity is key, even in cryptozoology!

o The Chupacabra, a cryptid often reported in Latin America, is described as a heavy creature, the size of a small bear, with spikes down its back. It's definitely not your typical pet.

o Mothman, a cryptid reportedly seen in West Virginia in the 1960s, is described as a man-sized creature with large reflective red eyes and wings. Sounds like a cross between a superhero and a horror movie!

o A classic example of a cryptid is the Jackalope, a mythical animal of North American folklore described as a jackrabbit with antelope horns or deer antlers. Now that's a hare-raising experience!

o The Kraken, a sea monster of gigantic size in Scandinavian folklore, is another popular cryptid. No calamari jokes, please!

o One of the most famous cryptids, Bigfoot, also known as Sasquatch, is often reported in North American forests. It's one big footstep for mankind!

o Cryptozoology has been criticized for its reliance on anecdotal information and lack of scientific methodology. However, this doesn't deter enthusiasts from seeking out the unknown.

o One common tool used by cryptozoologists is cast-making, where a plaster cast is made of a supposed cryptid footprint. CSI: Cryptid Scene Investigation!

o In 2014, a supposed "Chupacabra" was captured in Texas. However, DNA testing revealed it was just a raccoon with a skin disease. It's not easy being a cryptid.

- There's a Cryptozoology achievement in the video game World of Warcraft, awarded to players who track down various rare beasts. Unleash your inner cryptozoologist!
- It's not all about monsters. Some cryptozoologists hunt for out-of-place animals, like black panthers reported in non-native habitats. Always expect the unexpected in cryptozoology!

Chapter 11
The Loch Ness Monster
Uncovering the Truth Behind the Legend

- The Loch Ness Monster, affectionately known as Nessie, is said to inhabit Loch Ness, a large, deep, freshwater loch in the Scottish Highlands. It's got a pretty prestigious address!

- The first recorded sighting of Nessie was in 565 AD by St. Columba, who reportedly saved a man from being attacked by a water monster. Talk about an ancient neighborhood watch!

- The most famous photograph of Nessie, known as "The Surgeon's Photo," taken in 1934, was later revealed to be a hoax. Talk about a fishy story!

- There are several theories about what Nessie might be, ranging from a surviving plesiosaur to an enormous eel or even a misidentified bird or otter. Diversity at its finest!

- The Loch Ness Monster has become a significant attraction, with thousands of tourists visiting Loch Ness each year hoping to catch a glimpse of the elusive creature. Monster or not, Nessie's a star!

- In 1987, an operation called Project Deepscan used a fleet of 20 sonar-equipped boats to scan the depths of Loch Ness for Nessie. Despite some interesting readings, Nessie remained elusive. It's like playing hide and seek with a cryptid!

o Nessie's fame has spread globally, and the creature has appeared in countless books, films, and TV shows. That's one busy monster!

o Google celebrated the 81st anniversary of "The Surgeon's Photo" in 2015 with a Google Doodle and street-view images of Loch Ness. Even monsters get their own Google Doodle!

o Despite many expeditions and investigations, there's still no definitive evidence of Nessie's existence. However, hope springs eternal for Nessie enthusiasts!

o In 2019, scientists conducted a DNA study of the waters of Loch Ness. While they found no dinosaur DNA, they found a significant amount of eel DNA, suggesting Nessie might be a giant eel. Plot twist!

o The Loch Ness Monster has an estimated worth of £41 million per year for the Scottish economy. Who knew a cryptid could be such a cash cow?

o There's even a Loch Ness Marathon. If you're lucky, you might spot Nessie cheering from the water!

o Despite Nessie's fame, Loch Ness is an interesting place in its own right. It contains more water than all the lakes in England and Wales combined. That's one spacious home for Nessie!

o There are annual Nessie sightings reported to the Official Loch Ness Monster Sightings Register. Yes, there's an official register. Serious business!

o There's a theory that Nessie sightings could be due to seismic activity under Loch Ness causing large bubbles to rise to the surface, known as "gas ebullition." That's one way to make a splash!

o In the 1970s, Boston's Academy of Applied Science combined sonar and underwater photography in an attempt to find Nessie. While they captured some intriguing sonar readings and blurry photos, the evidence wasn't conclusive.

o The earliest report of a monster associated with the vicinity of Loch Ness appears in the Life of St. Columba by Adomnán, written in the 7th century. It's safe to say that Nessie is a legend with some serious staying power!

o Many Nessie believers think the monster looks like a plesiosaur, a type of long-necked marine dinosaur. However, skeptics note that the Loch was frozen solid during recent ice ages.

o Loch Ness is about 23 miles long and up to 1.5 miles wide, with a depth of up to 755 feet. That's a lot of room for Nessie to play hide-and-seek!

o Nessie is so famous that she's become a symbol of Scotland, appearing in various promotional materials and even having souvenirs made in her image. Not bad for a cryptid that's notoriously camera-shy!

Chapter 12
Bigfoot
Investigating Reports of This Elusive Creature

○ Bigfoot, also known as Sasquatch, is an ape-like creature that is said to inhabit the forests of North America. A true hide-and-seek champion!

○ The term "Sasquatch" originates from the Halkomelem word "sásq'ets," a language of indigenous peoples from the Pacific Northwest.

○ Bigfoot is often reported as being 6–9 feet tall and covered in dark hair, with footprints up to 24 inches long. With footprints that size, who needs a red carpet?

○ The first reported sightings of Bigfoot were from indigenous communities, with many Native American tribes having stories and traditions involving a large, hairy, man-like creature.

○ The Patterson-Gimlin film, shot in 1967 in California, remains one of the most famous pieces of evidence for Bigfoot's existence. It's one of the few times Bigfoot has had a starring role!

○ Despite numerous sightings and footprints, no Bigfoot remains have ever been found. Sasquatch: 1, Humanity: 0.

○ Bigfoot has a more urban relative: the Skunk Ape, which is reportedly seen in Florida, North Carolina, and Arkansas. Family reunion must be a hoot!

- There's a Bigfoot Field Researchers Organization (BFRO) that collects data on Bigfoot sightings and conducts research to validate its existence.
- The state of Washington has the highest number of Bigfoot sightings, closely followed by California. Bigfoot, it seems, prefers the West Coast!
- Bigfoot is known for its distinctive, unpleasant smell, described by witnesses as similar to skunk or rotten eggs. Apparently, Sasquatch isn't big on personal hygiene.
- In 2007, Bigfoot was declared "officially" non-existent by the Canadian government after a member of Parliament asked the government to ensure Bigfoot's protection.
- Yeti, Yowie, and Almas are international relatives of Bigfoot, according to local lore in the Himalayas, Australia, and Central Asia, respectively.
- Many believe Bigfoot is a Gigantopithecus, a large, prehistoric ape that lived in Asia and migrated to North America. Talk about a globe-trotter!
- There's even a "Bigfoot Scenic Byway" in California. Perfect for those who fancy a road trip with a side of cryptid hunting!
- Some states in the U.S., including Washington and Oregon, have proposed bills to protect Bigfoot. Bigfoot protection laws - you can't make this stuff up!
- There have been several alleged Bigfoot hoaxes, such as the infamous "Bigfoot in a freezer" hoax of 2008.
- "Finding Bigfoot" is a popular TV show on Animal Planet where a team of investigators attempt to find evidence of Bigfoot's existence. It's like a reality TV show for cryptozoologists!
- Bigfoot is such a cultural phenomenon that there's a North American festival dedicated to it. It includes guest speakers, live music, and Bigfoot calling contests.
- The lack of conclusive evidence hasn't deterred belief in Bigfoot. A 2012 poll found that up to 14% of Americans believe in Bigfoot. That's a lot of Bigfoot believers!
- Whether Bigfoot exists or not, it's undeniable that the creature has left a giant footprint (pun intended) on North American folklore and pop culture.

Chapter 13
The Chupacabra
Examining Sightings of the Goatsucker

- The name "Chupacabra" comes from Spanish and roughly translates to "goat-sucker," due to the creature's reported habit of attacking and drinking the blood of livestock. Quite a terrifying diet plan!

- Chupacabra first entered popular consciousness in the mid-1990s, following a rash of mysterious livestock deaths in Puerto Rico.

- Despite its relatively recent emergence, Chupacabra has quickly become one of the most famous cryptids, alongside Bigfoot and the Loch Ness Monster.

- Chupacabra descriptions vary but often feature a creature 4-5 feet tall, with red eyes, spikes down its back, and a very alien-like appearance. Fashion-forward in the monster world!

- While first reported in Puerto Rico, Chupacabra sightings have been reported as far north as Maine and as far south as Chile.

- Some believe Chupacabras are extraterrestrial beings due to their strange, alien-like characteristics. From sucking goat blood to possible alien - quite a leap!

- In July 2004, a rancher in Texas killed a strange, dog-like creature that many believed was a Chupacabra, but DNA tests identified it as a coyote with mange.

- Some propose that Chupacabra is the result of a secret U.S. government genetics experiment gone wrong. Conspiracy theories abound!

- There's even a "Chupacabracon," a gaming convention in Austin, Texas, where you can roll the dice to take down the mythical beast.

- Chupacabra has been a subject of several TV shows and movies, including an episode of "The X-Files" and the SyFy movie "Chupacabra vs. The Alamo." Talk about a creature with a knack for drama!

- The Chupacabra is so popular that it's even the state cryptid of Puerto Rico.

- Reports of Chupacabra attacks often coincide with periods of economic distress, leading some researchers to suggest that Chupacabra may serve as a symbol of hardship.

- In Russia, Chupacabra sightings often describe the creature as a kangaroo-like being with a crocodile skin. A fashion choice only a Chupacabra could love!

- Chupacabra is often linked with El Vampiro de Moca, a creature blamed for similar livestock deaths in Puerto Rico during the 1970s.

- There's a brand of Texas craft beer named after the Chupacabra. You might need a pint or two after a goat-sucker encounter!

- The lack of solid evidence hasn't stopped Chupacabra from being a favorite subject of cryptozoologists around the world.

- Despite numerous sightings, no physical evidence of the Chupacabra has been found. Elusive, isn't it?

- Chupacabra has become a symbol of the southwestern United States and Latin America, with its image used in all sorts of merchandise.

- Benjamin Radford's book "Tracking the Chupacabra" is considered one of the most comprehensive investigations into the Chupacabra phenomenon.

- Whether real or myth, Chupacabra serves as a chilling reminder that there's still a lot we don't know about the world around us. So, always keep an eye on your livestock!

Chapter 14
Psychokinesis
The Power of the Mind to Move Objects

- Psychokinesis, also known as telekinesis, is the alleged psychic ability to influence the physical world with the mind. Now, if only we could use this to clean the house!

- The term "telekinesis" was coined in 1890 by Russian spiritualist Alexander N. Aksakov, while "psychokinesis" was introduced by American parapsychologist J.B. Rhine in the 1930s.

- Psychokinesis has been a popular subject in fiction, with perhaps the most famous example being Carrie, the protagonist of Stephen King's novel of the same name.

- Despite many individuals claiming to possess psychokinetic abilities, there is no scientifically accepted evidence supporting the phenomenon. Where's a psychic spoon-bender when you need one?

- The famous Uri Geller claimed he could bend spoons with his mind, leading to a craze in the 1970s. He later admitted he used illusion techniques, although he maintains he has genuine psychic powers.

- Nina Kulagina, a Russian woman, gained notoriety in the 1960s for her alleged psychokinetic abilities, which included moving objects on a table without touching them. A psychic party trick, anyone?

- Some research in quantum physics has been interpreted to suggest that the observer can influence the outcome of an event. However, this is a contentious interpretation, and most scientists do not believe it provides evidence for psychokinesis.

- A variation of psychokinesis is called "micro-PK." It involves influencing electronic devices or the roll of dice – perfect for that Vegas trip!

- American parapsychologist J.B. Rhine first began studying psychokinesis in a laboratory setting in the 1930s using dice-rolling experiments.

- James Hydrick, a self-proclaimed psychic, gained fame in the 1980s for his ability to turn pages of a phone book with his mind. However, it was later revealed to be a trick involving blowing very subtly.

- Proponents of psychokinesis often cite the phenomenon of poltergeists, which are said to move objects and cause other disturbances, as potential evidence of unconscious psychokinetic ability.

- Swiss medium Anna Rasmussen was claimed to exhibit telekinetic powers during séances in the 1910s. She was said to have moved handkerchiefs and other small objects without physical contact.

- Telekinesis was famously demonstrated in the Star Wars franchise by Jedi knights using "The Force." If only mastering it were as easy as a movie montage!

- A scientific prize of one million dollars has been offered by the James Randi Educational Foundation for anyone who can demonstrate psychokinetic ability under controlled conditions. As of my knowledge cutoff in 2021, the prize has not been claimed.

- Psychokinesis even had a moment in the Olympics! In 1988, psychic spoon bender Uri Geller was invited to help Mexico's football team in a penalty shootout. Unfortunately, they still lost.

- Some researchers have proposed that certain unexplained phenomena, such as spontaneous human combustion, might be the result of uncontrolled psychokinesis.

- "Macro-PK" is a term for large-scale psychokinetic effects that can be seen with the naked eye.

- Telekinetic phenomena have often been reported in haunted locations. But are the ghosts moving the furniture, or is it a psychic visitor?

- Some psychic mediums claim they can help individuals develop their latent psychokinetic abilities. If only they could help find those missing keys!

- While many skeptics dismiss psychokinesis as mere illusion or trickery, it continues to captivate the public's imagination, fostering a sense of wonder about the untapped potential of the human mind. So, keep on thinking – who knows what might move!

Chapter 15
The Yeti
Searching for Evidence of the Abominable Snowman

o The Yeti, also known as the Abominable Snowman, is an ape-like creature said to inhabit the Himalayan region of Nepal, Bhutan, and Tibet. No word yet on if it's a fan of the cold!

o The term "Abominable Snowman" was coined in 1921 during a British Mount Everest expedition because of mistranslation of the Tibetan name "Metoh-Kangmi," which actually means "man-bear snow-man." Talk about a game of telephone!

o The Sherpa people of the Himalayas were the first to report sightings of the Yeti. Legend has it, the Yeti is a nocturnal creature that whistles and growls. Good luck getting a night's sleep with that serenade!

o While evidence of the Yeti is largely anecdotal, some physical proofs like tracks, hairs, and even supposed scalps and hands are preserved in monasteries or held by individuals. Yeti artifacts, anyone?

o The scientific community generally regards the Yeti as a legend, given the lack of conclusive evidence. But for those living in the Himalayas, the Yeti is very much part of their reality and folklore.

o Sir Edmund Hillary, the first confirmed mountaineer to summit Mount Everest, was reportedly involved in a Yeti expedition in 1960. They brought back a Yeti scalp from a monastery, later identified as being made from the skin of a serow – a Himalayan goat-like animal.

o There are several theories about what the Yeti could be if it does exist. Some suggest it might be a type of bear, while others think it could be a relic hominid like Gigantopithecus, a giant ape that lived thousands of years ago.

o The Yeti has left a substantial footprint (pun intended) on popular culture. It has featured in numerous films, TV shows, books, and video games. And let's not forget all those Yeti-themed souvenirs!

o The mountainous and inaccessible nature of the Yeti's supposed habitat in the Himalayas makes the search for it particularly challenging. It seems the Yeti isn't keen on visitors!

o In 2019, the Indian Army tweeted they'd found what they thought were Yeti tracks. However, experts suggested the prints were probably from a bear. Close, but no cigar!

o The Yeti is often likened to North America's Bigfoot or Sasquatch, although they are said to be distinct creatures. It seems every continent wants its own mysterious beast!

o Reinhold Messner, a renowned Italian mountaineer, conducted expeditions in the Himalayas during the 1980s. He reported encountering a creature that he initially thought was a Yeti, but later identified it as a bear that was walking upright.

o British mountaineer Don Whillans claimed to have witnessed a creature when scaling Annapurna in the 1970s. He said he heard some strange cries, saw dark shapes moving on two legs, and found footprints. A classic Yeti encounter, if you ask me!

o Tintin, the famous comic book character, had an adventure involving the Yeti titled "Tintin in Tibet." Talk about a hair-raising escapade!

o Some locals and monks believe that the Yeti has supernatural powers and is a god or a guardian of the mountains. It's not just a beast; it's a deity!

- Bhutan has a Yeti-themed park called the Sakteng Wildlife Sanctuary, primarily aimed at preserving the habitat of the mythical creature. Talk about Yeti conservation!

- Yeti is also the name of a popular brand of coolers and drinkware. However, there's no evidence to suggest that the Abominable Snowman enjoys cold drinks!

- The Yeti even has an official day to its name! December 5 is celebrated as International Yeti Day. So, mark your calendars for the most abominable party of the year!

- The 1951 Everest Expedition by Eric Shipton kick-started the Yeti craze in the Western world. Shipton photographed a number of large footprints in the snow, which he believed belonged to the "Abominable Snowman."

- Cryptozoologists continue to study and search for evidence of the Yeti's existence. The search for the elusive Snowman goes on – you could say it's snow joke for these enthusiasts!

Chapter 16
The Mothman
Investigating Sightings of This Winged Cryptid

- The Mothman is a creature reportedly seen in the Point Pleasant area of West Virginia from November 15, 1966, to December 15, 1967. It's been over 50 years, but this winged wonder still ruffles feathers!

- The first reported sighting of the Mothman was by five men who were digging a grave at a cemetery and saw something they described as a "brown human being" that flew out from some nearby trees. Talk about an uninvited guest!

- The Mothman is often described as a bipedal winged humanoid. Despite his name, he is in no way related to moths. A misnomer has never caused such a flap!

- The Mothman was popularized by John Keel's 1975 book, "The Mothman Prophecies," which linked the creature to various supernatural events and disasters. The book was later adapted into a movie starring Richard Gere.

- The Mothman is often associated with the collapse of the Silver Bridge in December 1967, a tragedy that resulted in the deaths of 46 people. Some residents claimed to have seen the Mothman near the bridge just before the collapse.

- The Mothman is celebrated annually at the Mothman Festival in Point Pleasant, which began in 2002. The festival features a variety of events such as guest speakers, vendor exhibits, and hayride tours focusing on the notable areas of Point Pleasant.

- The TNT Area, where the Mothman was often sighted in the 1960s, is now a tourist destination and wildlife management area. Perhaps the Mothman is an unofficial birdwatcher?

- A statue of the Mothman, complete with shiny red eyes, was erected in Point Pleasant in 2003. It's a must-see for fans of the winged enigma.

- In 2016, WCHS-TV published a photo purported to be of the Mothman. However, wildlife biologist Dr. Daniel Cristol said the image showed "a bird, with something in its mouth." A moth-eaten theory, indeed!

- The Mothman has been referenced in various media, including video games like "Fallout 76" set in West Virginia. It seems this winged creature is virtually unstoppable!

- The Mothman has been reportedly sighted in other parts of the world as well, including outside a mine in Freiburg, Germany, before a mine collapse. It seems our creature has a frequent flyer card!

- Some theories suggest the Mothman could be an undiscovered species of large bird or possibly a misidentified or mutated known species. Ornithologists, the game is afoot!

- The Mothman is considered a harbinger of doom by some, appearing before disasters. Kind of like a very ominous weather forecast!

- Cryptozoologists, who study entities from folklore like the Mothman, have yet to find hard evidence of its existence. But the search continues. After all, it's a moth-eat-moth world out there!

- There's a Mothman Museum in Point Pleasant for those who want to delve deeper into the lore, the sightings, and the impact of the Mothman. This is truly where the Mothman fandom flocks together!

- Some believe the Mothman might be an alien or extraterrestrial being, given its peculiar physical attributes and the unusual occurrences surrounding its sightings. He just might be the most alien of all the bird species!

- There's a theory that the Mothman could be a product of the region's high pollution levels, resulting from nearby munitions manufacturing sites. Guess even legendary creatures can't escape environmental issues!

- The Mothman isn't the only mysterious creature reported in West Virginia. The state is also known for sightings of the Flatwoods Monster and the White Thing. Let's just say, West Virginia is a cryptid's paradise!

- Sightings of the Mothman have inspired a wealth of creative works, including books, films, music, and even an episode of the TV show "Supernatural." It's safe to say, the Mothman has landed... in pop culture!

- The Mothman's red eyes are one of its most distinctive features. Some eyewitnesses have said that just looking into them instilled intense fear. Looks like the Mothman has a truly eye-catching presence!

Chapter 17
ESP and Telepathy
The Science of Mind Reading

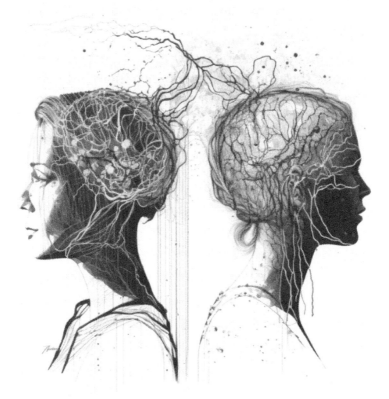

- ESP, or extrasensory perception, is sometimes called the "sixth sense." It includes claimed reception of information not gained through the recognized physical senses. Mind-blowing, isn't it?

- The term "telepathy" was coined in 1882 by the psychologist Frederic W. H. Myers, a founder of the Society for Psychical Research. It derives from the Greek "tele," meaning "distant," and "patheia," meaning "feeling." So, telepathy could be interpreted as "distant-feeling." Pass the feeling, anyone?

- American psychologist Joseph Banks Rhine is often credited with popularizing the term "ESP" and conducting extensive laboratory tests to quantify psychic phenomena. His results, however, have often been criticized for lack of scientific rigor. Rhine or not, the debate continues!

- The U.S. government had a program for investigating psychic phenomena for military purposes known as Stargate Project. The results? Inconclusive. Perhaps they should have seen that coming?

- In ESP, information is said to be received without using any of our known sensory channels or physical interaction. No need for Wi-Fi here!

- There have been instances where twins reportedly share a telepathic connection, often feeling each other's pain or emotions, even when they're miles apart. It's a twintuition!

- Parapsychology is the study of paranormal and psychic phenomena, including ESP and telepathy. It's a field that's often met with skepticism and controversy in the scientific community. Say it loud, parapsychologists: We believe!

- Some animals are believed to have ESP or telepathic abilities, often sensing danger before it happens. Pets or psychic companions? You decide!

- The Global Consciousness Project, also known as the EGG Project, studies the potential for human consciousness to express itself as a global field. The project uses electronic devices, known as "eggs," placed around the world to collect data. Any scrambled signals, anyone?

- Zener cards, a deck of 25 cards featuring five different symbols, were used in the early 20th century for experimental research into ESP. Shuffle up and deal some psychic vibes!

- A well-known alleged telepath was Nina Kulagina, a Russian woman filmed apparently moving objects without touch in the 1960s. Onlookers were blown away, metaphorically speaking!

- Telepathy is a common trope in science fiction and superhero stories. From Marvel's Jean Grey to Star Trek's Vulcans, mind-reading abilities make for fantastic plotlines!

- Sigmund Freud, the father of psychoanalysis, showed a keen interest in telepathy and wrote of its potential existence in his work. Imagine getting into Freud's head!

- A "Ganzfeld experiment" is a technique used in the field of parapsychology to test individuals for extrasensory perception. It involves sensory deprivation to enhance the mind's receptivity. It's quiet... maybe too quiet!

- Some skeptics attribute claims of ESP to cognitive biases like the confirmation bias, where individuals favor information that confirms their existing beliefs. Whether you believe in ESP or not, you're bound to find evidence that suits you!

- There's a claim that everyone possesses ESP abilities, but they remain dormant or underdeveloped in most individuals. Psychic or not, we all have untapped potential!

- Some researchers have suggested that telepathy occurs most frequently in dreams. So next time you dream of someone, remember, you might just be tuning into their frequency!

- In the 1970s, a popular ESP test involved sender-receiver experiments with pictures. The receiver would attempt to draw or describe the image the sender was looking at. A picture's worth a thousand psychic words!

- Telepathy has been reported among very close family members or friends. It seems that the closer the bond, the stronger the telepathic connection.

- Psychokinesis is often confused with telepathy, but they're different. While telepathy is about reading minds or transferring thoughts, psychokinesis involves moving objects with the mind. It's all in your head!

Chapter 18
The Jersey Devil
Exploring the Legend of This Mysterious Creature

o The Jersey Devil is a legendary creature said to inhabit the Pine Barrens of South Jersey. With its reported horse-like head, wings, and devilish features, it's not exactly the kind of animal you'd want to encounter on a forest walk.

o The legend of the Jersey Devil dates back to the 1700s. Its origin story involves a woman named Mother Leeds who cursed her 13th child, transforming it into a monstrous creature that flew out of the chimney. Talk about a dramatic exit!

o The state of New Jersey is so proud of its devilish folklore that they even named a professional hockey team after it - the New Jersey Devils. Ice hockey with a side of mythical beasts, anyone?

o The Jersey Devil is also known as the Leeds Devil, named after the Leeds family with which the creature's origin story is associated. How would you like a mythical monster named after your family?

o In January 1909, there was a flurry of reported sightings of the Jersey Devil, causing widespread panic and even school closures across the state. Now that's what I call a school snow... I mean, devil day!

o Cryptozoologists, those who study animals whose existence is not yet proven, continue to search for evidence of the Jersey Devil. There's a job that won't ever get boring!

- Despite the ominous name, the Jersey Devil has been more of a nuisance than a threat in its legend. It's been blamed for raiding chicken coops and scaring locals, but it's not known for more serious devilish deeds.

- Napoleon Bonaparte's older brother, Joseph, allegedly saw the Jersey Devil while living in Bordentown, New Jersey, in the early 19th century. Apparently, even ex-kings aren't immune to local hauntings!

- One of the most famous alleged encounters with the Jersey Devil was by Joseph Bonaparte, the elder brother of Napoleon Bonaparte. That's one way to make a history lesson more exciting!

- Not all Jersey Devil sightings describe the creature in the same way. Some accounts suggest it has a dog-like face, while others describe it as looking more like a horse or a kangaroo. Perhaps the Jersey Devil is a shapeshifter?

- Despite numerous sightings, no physical evidence of the Jersey Devil has ever been found. The mystery continues!

- The Jersey Devil has been featured in various forms of media, from books to video games. It's even been an episode plot for TV shows like "The X-Files."

- Burlington, New Jersey, holds an annual "Jersey Devil & Fable Festival," celebrating the state's legendary creature with activities, live music, and more. Party with the Devil, anyone?

- The Pine Barrens, the supposed home of the Jersey Devil, is a vast forested area that covers over 1 million acres. If the Jersey Devil is hiding there, it's got plenty of space!

- The Jersey Devil legend is so well-known in the local area that there's even a Jersey Devil-themed wine from the Tomasello Winery in Hammonton, NJ. A sip of the unknown, anyone?

- Despite its fearsome reputation, the Jersey Devil has become a popular mascot. There are even cute, cuddly Jersey Devil plush toys. Who wouldn't want to snuggle up with a legendary beast?

- Some theories suggest the Jersey Devil could be a misidentified creature, like a sandhill crane, which can have a wingspan of almost 7 feet. From devil to bird, that's quite a downgrade!

- The Leeds family, with whom the Jersey Devil legend is associated, had a family crest featuring a dragon-like creature. Some suggest this could be the source of the Jersey Devil myth. That's one way to start a family legend!

o   Merchants Millpond State Park in North Carolina has a canoe trail named after the Jersey Devil, the "Lassiter Trail". Paddle at your own risk!

o   The legend of the Jersey Devil has been used to promote conservation efforts in the Pine Barrens, a unique and precious ecosystem. Spooky tales for a good cause, that's eco-friendly haunting!

Chapter 19
The Black Dahlia
Investigating the Murder and Possible Supernatural Connections

o The Black Dahlia is the nickname given to Elizabeth Short, a woman who was brutally murdered in Los Angeles in 1947. Her unsolved case has intrigued crime enthusiasts for decades.

o The name "Black Dahlia" was inspired by a film noir murder mystery, "The Blue Dahlia," which was released just a year before Elizabeth Short's death. This certainly added an extra layer of mystique to the case.

o Despite popular belief, Elizabeth Short was not known as the "Black Dahlia" during her lifetime. The nickname was a posthumous creation by the media.

o The case of the Black Dahlia is famous not just for its brutality, but also for its mystery. Despite numerous suspects, the crime remains unsolved to this day. Talk about a cold case!

o Elizabeth Short was an aspiring actress, which only added to the Hollywood allure and tragic glamour of her story. Dreaming of stardom, she instead became infamous.

- One of the reasons the Black Dahlia case became so famous was due to the media circus that followed. Sensational headlines and lurid details were splashed across newspapers, stoking public curiosity and fear.

- Several people confessed to the murder of the Black Dahlia over the years, but none of these confessions were ever proven. Seems like some people will do anything for a bit of notoriety.

- The body of Elizabeth Short was found severed at the waist and drained of blood, a gruesome detail that added to the horror of the Black Dahlia case. It's no wonder it has continued to fascinate crime enthusiasts and historians.

- There have been numerous books and films inspired by the Black Dahlia case, further cementing its place in the annals of American crime history.

- The murder site where Elizabeth Short's body was found is located in a residential area of Los Angeles, now known as Leimert Park. How's that for a grim claim to fame?

- Despite its gruesome history, the Black Dahlia case has been heavily romanticized in popular culture, often depicted with a certain noir-esque glamour that belies the reality of Elizabeth Short's tragic death.

- One of the most infamous suspects in the Black Dahlia case was Dr. George Hodel, whose own son, a former LAPD detective, accused him of the murder years later. Family dinners must have been awkward after that!

- Over the years, the Black Dahlia case has been linked to various other unsolved murders and crimes, though no definitive connections have been made.

- Elizabeth Short was only 22 when she was murdered, a fact that contributed to the tragedy and shock of the Black Dahlia case.

- The Black Dahlia case was one of the first to be heavily covered by the media, setting a precedent for the sensationalist reporting of violent crimes.

- The last person known to have seen Elizabeth Short alive was Robert "Red" Manley, a married salesman who admitted to having had a date with her. However, he was cleared of suspicion by the police.

- Despite endless speculation, investigations, and media coverage, the Black Dahlia murder remains one of Los Angeles' most infamous unsolved crimes.

- The Black Dahlia case remains a favorite among true crime enthusiasts and is frequently referenced in books, podcasts, and documentaries.
- Not only is the Black Dahlia murder one of the most famous unsolved cases in LA history, but it also has its own dedicated tours, taking visitors to all the key locations related to the crime.
- The story of the Black Dahlia is a tragic reminder of the dark side of Hollywood's glamour and glitz, a stark contrast to the city's sunny facade.

Chapter 20
The Real Amityville Horror
Examining the Legend Behind the Infamous Haunted House

- The Amityville Horror is a famous haunted house tale that inspired numerous movies and books, most notably Jay Anson's 1977 book "The Amityville Horror: A True Story."

- The house at the center of the Amityville Horror story is a real place, located at 112 Ocean Avenue, Amityville, New York. However, the street number has since been changed to keep the curious away.

- The chilling tale of the Amityville Horror began with the gruesome murder of the DeFeo family in 1974, carried out by the eldest son, Ronald DeFeo Jr. All six members of the family were killed in their sleep.

- Just a year after the DeFeo murders, the Lutz family moved into the Amityville house and claimed to experience a series of paranormal occurrences, which included strange noises, sudden temperature drops, and even oozing green slime!

- The Lutz family lasted only 28 days in the Amityville house before leaving due to the alleged hauntings. How's that for a quick change of address?

- George Lutz, the head of the Lutz family, claimed that he would wake up at 3:15 AM every morning, the exact time Ronald DeFeo Jr. said he carried out the murders.

- Among the various alleged happenings in the Amityville house, the Lutz family reported seeing a demonic pig-like creature with glowing red eyes. Now, that's not something you want to find in your piggy bank!

- The Amityville house is a five-bedroom Dutch Colonial style home, and its distinctive gambrel roof has made it an iconic image in horror culture.

- The events of the Amityville Horror have been hotly debated, with skeptics suggesting that the Lutz family invented the haunting to cash in on the house's tragic history.

- Despite the controversy surrounding the veracity of the Lutz family's claims, the Amityville Horror story has proven enduringly popular, spawning a lucrative horror franchise.

- The infamous red room in the basement of the Amityville house, a small room painted completely red, was said to be a hotbed of paranormal activity.

- A key figure in the Amityville Horror story is Ed and Lorraine Warren, famous paranormal investigators who visited the house and claimed it was occupied by malevolent spirits.

- The infamous Amityville house was put up for sale in 2016, with an asking price of $850,000. That's a hefty price tag for a piece of haunted history!

- The original Amityville Horror book was so popular that it was made into a film just two years after its release, in 1979.

- Over the years, there have been numerous lawsuits related to the Amityville Horror, including disputes over the story's veracity and the rights to the narrative.

- In an interesting twist, the Lutz children have given conflicting accounts of their time in the Amityville house, adding another layer of mystery to this already enigmatic story.

- Despite the change of address and numerous owners, the Amityville house has retained its infamous reputation and continues to be a magnet for horror enthusiasts.

- The Lutz family insisted that their experiences in the Amityville house were genuine, despite widespread skepticism and controversy.

- The 1979 film adaptation of the Amityville Horror was a huge box office success, grossing over $86 million and becoming one of the highest-grossing independent films of all time.

- Today, the Amityville Horror remains one of the most famous haunted house stories in America, its name synonymous with terror and mystery, and its enduring popularity is testament to our fascination with the supernatural and the unknown. Whether fact or fiction, it serves as a chilling reminder that sometimes, home is where the haunt is!

Chapter 21

Poltergeists

The Terrifying Reality Behind These Mischievous Spirits

- The term "poltergeist" comes from the German words "poltern," meaning to make a noise, and "geist," meaning ghost. Therefore, a poltergeist is a "noisy ghost." Quite the loud and proud personality, if you ask me.

- In paranormal lore, poltergeists are often associated with adolescent girls. This has led some to believe that the kinetic energy produced during puberty might be the cause of this phenomenon. Puberty is hard enough without adding ghosts into the mix!

- The Enfield Poltergeist case in the UK is one of the most well-known and heavily investigated. The occurrences were so violent and frequent that they were witnessed by police, neighbors, and journalists. Talk about a busy household!

- In contrast to many ghostly encounters, poltergeists are known for their physical interactions. They don't just passively spook you; they throw objects, move furniture, and even slap or bite. They're not ones for subtlety!

- The movie "Poltergeist" (1982) was so influential that many people believe the film set was cursed due to the use of real human skeletons as props. In the years following, several cast members experienced untimely deaths, fueling the belief in the "Poltergeist Curse."

- Poltergeist activity is often short-lived, usually lasting a few weeks to a few months. One theory is that these spirits have a limited energy source and eventually "burn out." Guess even ghosts need a recharge!

- The Borley Rectory in England is dubbed "the most haunted house in England" due to the intense poltergeist activity reported there, which included phantom writing appearing on the walls. Who needs a pen and paper when you have a wall and a ghost?

- Reports of poltergeist activity date back to ancient Roman times. One account tells of a ghost that tormented a family by throwing stones, moving furniture, and starting fires. Not exactly the most considerate houseguest, huh?

- The Bell Witch, a famous American poltergeist tale, involved a spirit that could mimic voices and had a particular fondness for singing hymns. Hymns and hauntings, a match made in... well, not heaven, surely!

- Some parapsychologists propose that poltergeist activity could be the result of "spontaneous psychokinesis," where a living person unknowingly manipulates physical objects using their mind. Imagine having that kind of power and not knowing it!

- The phenomenon of "exploding head syndrome," where a person is startled awake by a loud noise that doesn't actually exist, has sometimes been attributed to poltergeist activity. But really, wouldn't we all explode if we were awakened too early?

- The Rosenheim Poltergeist case in Germany involved strange phone call incidents. Callers reported hearing strange music and noises on the line, and the telephone bill was inflated due to numerous calls to the speaking clock. Now that's a long-distance relationship you don't want!

- Some famous poltergeist cases have occurred in schools. The South Shields Poltergeist in the UK was reported to leave messages on a child's electronic toy. Looks like somebody needs to go back to ghost school!

- In many cultures, poltergeists are believed to be mischievous spirits of the deceased or supernatural entities like demons. But don't worry, they're just trying to make some noise in the afterlife.

- Some poltergeists appear to have a favorite object to move or throw. In the Mackenzie Poltergeist case in Scotland, it was reportedly fond of throwing stones and other objects at visitors. I guess everyone needs a hobby!

- Poltergeist cases often end as suddenly as they began, with no apparent reason or pattern. The chaotic energy of a poltergeist is much like a storm, coming and going as it pleases.

- During the famous case of the Epworth Rectory Poltergeist in the 18th century, the supposed spirit was named "Old Jeffrey" by the family it was tormenting. When life gives you poltergeists, name them and make them a part of the family!

- According to some accounts, poltergeists have been known to speak or convey messages. In the case of the Bell Witch, the spirit had conversations with the family. If only all house guests were that engaging!

- In pop culture, poltergeists are often portrayed as malevolent spirits, causing fear and harm. However, in real reported cases, while they can be mischievous and disruptive, they are rarely harmful.

- While some parapsychologists believe in the existence of poltergeists, there is no scientific evidence to support the phenomenon. But who needs science when you have a good ghost story, right?

Chapter 22
Near-Death Experiences
What Happens When We Cross Over to the Other Side

o Near-death experiences (NDEs) often include a feeling of peace, a sensation of floating outside the body, moving through a tunnel, or meeting deceased loved ones. Seems like quite the trip!

o NDEs are reported across cultures and religions, showing remarkable similarities regardless of personal beliefs. Talk about a universal vacation package!

o The term "near-death experience" was coined by Dr. Raymond Moody in his 1975 book "Life After Life." This book brought widespread attention to the phenomenon.

o An estimated 4-15% of people have had an NDE. So, you could be part of an exclusive club, just by nearly dying!

o Some people report hyperreal and vivid memories from their NDEs, sometimes with more clarity than any of their earthly experiences. Can you imagine remembering your near-death vacation better than your actual one?

o Many people report a life review during their NDE, in which they see and re-experience major and minor events of their lives. Who needs a photo album when you have a near-death experience?

o Following an NDE, many people report changes in their personalities, such as being more compassionate, having a reduced fear of death, and a higher sense of purpose. It's like extreme self-improvement!

o Some individuals with NDEs describe a border or a boundary that signifies a point of no return. It's like being at the edge of the world, but even more so.

o People blind from birth have reported visual experiences during their NDEs. Now, that's what I call a sight for sore eyes!

o There's a Near Death Experience Research Foundation (NDERF) that collects and studies NDE stories from around the world. Talk about a fascinating job!

o Some individuals who have had an NDE describe a rapid, almost instant, travel to other realms. If only we could do that to avoid traffic!

o A study found that people who have had NDEs are more likely to believe in life after death than those who haven't. Well, if you've seen the "other side," why wouldn't you?

o Dr. Eben Alexander, a neurosurgeon, claimed to have had an NDE while in a coma, and he wrote a bestselling book about it, "Proof of Heaven." Not everyone can claim to have seen heaven and come back to write a book about it!

o The first medical book on NDEs, "Recollections of Death: A Medical Perspective," was written by Dr. Michael Sabom, a cardiologist. He interviewed patients who had experienced clinical death and were later revived.

o There are reports of NDE experiencers meeting beings of light, often described as loving and welcoming. It's like a spiritual welcoming committee!

o Some scientists believe that NDEs may be the result of the brain releasing endorphins to reduce pain and stress. Or it might be due to certain drugs or a dying brain's last hurrah.

o Despite the name, you don't have to be close to death to have a near-death experience. Some people have reported NDEs during meditation, extreme physical exertion, or even sleep!

- NDE experiencers often report a profound sense of understanding or universal knowledge during the experience. Unfortunately, this typically fades upon returning to the earthly realm. If only we could remember the secrets of the universe!

- There's even an International Association for Near-Death Studies (IANDS), which holds conferences and publishes a peer-reviewed journal. If you've ever wanted to delve into the mysterious world of NDEs, this is the place to start!

- Many skeptics argue that NDEs are a type of lucid dream or hallucination triggered by physiological processes, but for those who have experienced them, they are incredibly real and transformative. One man's dream could be another's reality, after all!

Chapter 23
Ouija Boards
Separating Fact from Fiction About This Infamous Tool of the Occult

o The name "Ouija" is believed to be a combination of the French and German words for "yes" – oui and ja. Talk about bilingual communication with the other side!

o The Ouija board got its patent in 1891, and the patent office only granted it after the board correctly spelled out the patent officer's name. That must have been one spook-tacular interview!

o Critics argue that the movements of the planchette (the small heart-shaped piece that moves around the board) are actually due to the ideomotor effect – subconscious movements made by the people using the board. So, maybe it's not the spirits spelling out "HELLO" but your best friend pranking you?

o While often associated with occultism today, Ouija boards were initially marketed as a fun parlor game. Talk about your game night taking a dark turn!

o Some people believe that using a Ouija board can accidentally invite malevolent spirits or open a doorway for demonic possession. Might not be the best choice for a kid's birthday party, then.

- In 1993, the Baltimore building where Ouija boards were first manufactured was ironically converted into a 7-Eleven convenience store. Wonder if the slurpee machine is haunted?

- There is a superstition that Ouija boards must be "disposed of" properly, or they can return to haunt the owner. Methods include breaking the board into seven pieces, sprinkling it with holy water, and burying it. Sounds like a lot of work for a board game!

- Ouija boards have made appearances in numerous films and TV shows, most famously in "The Exorcist" where it was blamed for the main character's possession. Talk about bad publicity!

- Some famous people have used Ouija boards – including Bill Wilson, the co-founder of Alcoholics Anonymous, who claimed to have written some of his work with the help of a spirit contacted via the board.

- The largest Ouija board in the world, "Ouijazilla," was unveiled in Salem, Massachusetts, in 2019. It is 3,168 square feet and weighs 9,000 pounds. Now that's a big "HELLO" from the other side!

- Despite their spooky reputation, Ouija boards are currently sold by toy and game companies and are recommended for ages eight and up. Remember when your biggest worry was whether you'd land on "Park Place" in Monopoly?

- Some mediums and psychic researchers refuse to use Ouija boards, believing they attract low-level spirits or "astral junk."

- In World War I, Pearl Curran, a St. Louis housewife, began using the Ouija board and claimed to have contacted a spirit named Patience Worth. The two allegedly co-authored several novels, poetry and prose, which were celebrated by the literary community at the time.

- Some people believe that you should never use a Ouija board alone, as it makes you more susceptible to potential negative spiritual influences.

- An interesting rule often followed by users is to never let the planchette move to the four corners of the board, as it is believed that it can release an evil spirit.

- It is considered bad luck to leave the planchette on the board when you are not using it. So, it's kind of like leaving your keys in the car?

- Some paranormal researchers suggest that if the planchette moves to spell the word "ZEUS" in a figure eight or count down from ten to one, you should immediately end the session by moving the planchette to "GOODBYE."

o The "Zozo" phenomenon relates to alleged encounters with a malevolent entity named Zozo during Ouija board sessions. Some users suggest avoiding any spirit that identifies by this name.

o Despite fears and criticisms, there is no scientific evidence to date that confirms the ability of Ouija boards to contact spirits or predict the future.

o Aleister Crowley, a famous occultist, was reported to use a Ouija board, and even wrote an entire book about the "Egyptian" tarot based on information he claimed to have received from the board.

Chapter 24
Curses
Investigating the Power and Reality of These Mystical Spells

o One of the most famous curses in history is the curse of the pharaohs. According to legend, anyone who disturbs the tomb of an ancient Egyptian pharaoh will be cursed with death or disaster. This became particularly popular after several members of Howard Carter's team died following the opening of Tutankhamun's tomb in 1922.

o The Hope Diamond, now housed in the Smithsonian Natural History Museum, is believed to carry a curse, bringing misfortune and tragedy to those who own or wear it. Its colorful history includes owners who went insane, were murdered, or committed suicide. A gem of a curse, isn't it?

o The curse of the Billy Goat on the Chicago Cubs baseball team originated in 1945 when a man and his pet goat were kicked out of the World Series game. The Cubs didn't win another World Series until 2016, breaking the 71-year "curse."

o The "27 Club" refers to a group of famous musicians who all died at the age of 27, leading some to speculate about a "curse." Members include Jimi Hendrix, Janis Joplin, Jim Morrison, and Kurt Cobain.

- The curse of Tippecanoe (or Tecumseh's curse) was a pattern noted by Ripley's Believe It or Not where presidents of the United States elected or re-elected in a year ending in zero (from William Henry Harrison in 1840 to John F. Kennedy in 1960) died in office.

- The Kennedy family is often said to be plagued by the "Kennedy Curse," due to the numerous tragedies and untimely deaths that have befallen them.

- There's a superstition in theater that saying the name of Shakespeare's "Macbeth" inside a theater will bring disaster. The correct etiquette is to refer to it as "The Scottish Play."

- The "Curse of the Bambino" refers to the 86-year period from 1918 to 2004 when the Boston Red Sox did not win a World Series. The curse supposedly began when the Red Sox sold Babe Ruth to the New York Yankees.

- The "Sports Illustrated Cover Jinx" refers to the superstition that an individual or team featured on the magazine's cover will subsequently experience bad luck or a slump in performance.

- King Louis XIV of France supposedly cursed the position of the Governor of the Bastille. After his appointment, each governor would meet a miserable end within a few years.

- The tomb of Tamerlane, a 14th-century Turco-Mongol conqueror, carried an inscription stating that whoever disturbed his rest would unleash an invader more fearsome than he. When Soviet anthropologists exhumed his body in 1941, Nazi Germany invaded the Soviet Union within hours.

- The "Curse of the Ninth" is a superstition among composers, where they fear to write their ninth symphony because they might die soon after, just like Beethoven, Schubert, and Mahler. Talk about performance pressure!

- The Otsuka family in Japan is said to be cursed for 20 generations due to an ancestor's sacrilege. The family supposedly suffers from terrible luck and has a history of unusual deaths.

- The "Oscar love curse" refers to a pattern where actresses win an Academy Award for Best Actress or Best Supporting Actress and then undergo relationship troubles or a breakup.

- It's believed that if you take black volcanic rocks from Hawaii Volcanoes National Park, you'll be cursed by Pele, the Hawaiian goddess of fire and volcanoes, until you return them.

- According to legend, the city of Timbuktu in Mali is cursed and anyone who takes anything from the city will be plagued with misfortune until the item is returned.

- Some believe that the "curse of the pharaohs" extends to the Titanic. The ship was carrying an Egyptian mummy when it sank, leading to speculation about a curse.

- A tale from Devon, England speaks of the "Cursed Purple Sapphire," also known as the Delhi Purple Sapphire, which supposedly brings disaster to anyone who owns it.

- Some people believe the cryptic Voynich manuscript carries a curse, causing anyone who attempts to decode it to become obsessed to the point of madness.

- The Romans had a form of curse tablet called "defixiones." These were small tablets inscribed with curses to be placed in the graves of the departed to compel the spirits to fulfill the curse.

Chapter 25
The Bell Witch
Examining the Legend of This Terrifying Poltergeist

o The Bell Witch is a famous Southern ghost story about a poltergeist that haunted the Bell family in Adams, Tennessee, in the early 19th century.

o The haunting began with strange noises in the house, like rats gnawing on bedposts and chains being dragged across the floor.

o The ghost was believed to have a particular dislike for the family patriarch, John Bell. It reportedly tormented him relentlessly and even claimed to have been the cause of his death.

o The Bell Witch was said to be able to mimic people's voices, move objects, and even physically assault people.

o The entity referred to itself as a witch and claimed to be named "Kate." Hence, it was often called "Kate the Bell's Witch."

o The future U.S. president, Andrew Jackson, allegedly visited the Bell homestead to see the witch for himself. His carriage wheels supposedly stopped mysteriously, and he's reported to have said, "By the eternal, boys, it is the witch."

o The Bell Witch was apparently highly intelligent and aware of things happening far from the Bell home. She once accurately detailed a sermon being given many miles away, baffling those who heard her recount it.

- One of the daughter Betsy Bell's biggest tormentors was said to be the witch herself, who apparently disapproved of her engagement to a local man named Joshua Gardner.

- The Bell Witch haunting is one of the few cases where a spirit's activity directly led to a person's death - John Bell's. Kate the Witch allegedly poisoned him.

- According to legend, the witch left the Bell family in 1821 with a promise to return in seven years. She reportedly did return in 1828 to Lucy Bell, but her antics were not as violent as before.

- The Bell Witch Cave, located on the family's land, is believed to be one of the places where the witch resided. It's now a tourist attraction.

- Some theories suggest that the Bell Witch was actually a manifestation of a Native American spirit angry at the land's desecration.

- John Bell's grave is the only one in the family cemetery that has a concrete slab over it. It's believed this was done to prevent the Bell Witch from haunting his remains.

- The Bell Witch inspired many cultural works, including films like "An American Haunting" and "The Blair Witch Project," and music like the Mercyful Fate song "The Bell Witch."

- According to legend, the witch claimed she would return in 107 years. In 1935, a new set of hauntings began in Adams, Tennessee, which some believed were her doing.

- Although the main events of the Bell Witch haunting occurred between 1817 and 1821, odd occurrences and unexplainable phenomena still happen in the area surrounding the old Bell farm.

- When the spirit was asked who it was and where it was from, it replied with a variety of answers, including that it was the witch of a neighbor woman, Kate Batts.

- The spirit exhibited a strong knowledge of the Bible, despite claiming to be a witch.

- It's been suggested that Betsy Bell herself was the witch, unconsciously controlling the phenomena through her own psychic abilities.

- The tale of the Bell Witch remains one of America's most chilling and enduring ghost stories. The tale serves as a cautionary parable about the dangers of allowing superstition and fear to rule one's life.

Chapter 26

Haunted Dolls

The Truth Behind These Infamous Toys

o   The concept of haunted dolls has been around for centuries, with many cultures believing that spirits can attach themselves to objects, including dolls.

o   Perhaps the most famous haunted doll is Robert the Doll, a straw-stuffed effigy that many believe is cursed. Robert is currently in a museum in Key West, Florida, where he is visited by tourists who hope to avoid his curse.

o   Legend says that you should always ask Robert the Doll for permission before taking his photo. If you don't, he'll curse you, and bad luck will follow.

o   The Annabelle doll, now locked in the Warren's Occult Museum in Connecticut, is said to be haunted by the spirit of a young girl. Annabelle's story has inspired a series of horror films.

o   Okiku is a haunted doll that resides in Japan. According to local legends, the doll's hair grows continually, even though it is made of ceramic and has no living cells.

- Mandy the Doll, residing in the Quesnel Museum in British Columbia, is said to cause strange activities. Electronic devices malfunction around her, and she apparently moves around by herself.

- The "Island of the Dolls" in Mexico is a well-known tourist spot where hundreds of dolls hang from trees. The dolls are said to be possessed by the spirit of a girl who drowned there.

- Some haunted dolls are sold online, with sellers claiming that they're inhabited by everything from the spirits of witches to demonic entities. Buyers beware!

- It's said that the spirit of a 7-year-old boy named Bobby inhabits a doll named "Charley." The owners reported hearing giggling and found the doll in different positions and locations.

- Haunted dolls are not only found in Western cultures. In Japan, a traditional doll known as a tsukumogami can become alive after 100 years.

- Some people are collectors of haunted dolls. They either enjoy the thrill of possibly experiencing supernatural phenomena or believe they can help the spirits find peace.

- Many psychics claim that dolls, like houses, can become haunted when their previous owners imprint their emotional or spiritual energy onto them.

- The "Devil Baby Doll" legend of New Orleans tells of a cursed doll that brings misfortune to anyone who possesses it.

- Peggy the Doll is believed to cause headaches, chest pains, and even hallucinations to those who look at her picture online.

- Letta the Gypsy Doll, found in Australia, is said to move on its own, change positions while seated, and even emit a pulse while being held.

- Some haunted dolls, like Joliet, are said to induce nightmares. Joliet's previous owner reported dreaming of the doll turning into a malevolent figure who commanded him to murder his family.

- Not all haunted dolls are old. Factory-made dolls from the 20th century, such as composition dolls, have also been reported as haunted.

- Harold the Doll was bought at a flea market and is considered one of the most haunted dolls in the world. He supposedly causes pain, injury, and bad luck to those who come in contact with him.

- Many haunted dolls reside in museums, such as the Zak Bagans' Haunted Museum in Las Vegas, which houses multiple allegedly haunted dolls.

- Some people believe that treating haunted dolls with respect, like asking for permission before taking their photos or moving them, can help prevent any supernatural retaliation.

Chapter 27
The Enfield Poltergeist
Investigating One of the Most Famous Cases of Paranormal Activity

- The Enfield Poltergeist is one of the most well-documented alleged cases of poltergeist activity, occurring between 1977 and 1979 in Enfield, London.

- The events focused around two young sisters, Janet and Margaret Hodgson, who lived in a council house with their mother and two brothers.

- Many skeptics point to the fact that much of the most extraordinary activity happened when the girls were alone or out of direct sight, leading some to believe they were clever pranksters.

- The first reported incident involved the two girls hearing shuffling noises in their bedroom and furniture moving of its own accord.

- At the height of the phenomena, Janet was reportedly levitated and thrown across the room, an event witnessed by neighbors and a police officer.

- One of the most chilling aspects of the case was the guttural voice that supposedly came from Janet. This voice identified itself as Bill, a previous resident of the house who died there.

- The Society for Psychical Research's investigator Maurice Grosse and author Guy Lyon Playfair, who spent a considerable amount of time with the family, were convinced of the legitimacy of the phenomena.

- The levitation of Janet Hodgson was captured in a photograph, which has become one of the iconic images of the Enfield Poltergeist. However, skeptics argue that it simply shows Janet jumping off the bed.

- In one famous incident, a police officer signed an affidavit stating she saw a chair move unaided across the floor of the living room.

- Janet, the most affected by the phenomena, was tested for psychokinetic abilities by various researchers, but no such capabilities were found.

- The haunting ceased in 1979, as suddenly as they had begun, and Janet left the house. She has since led a private life but maintains that the events were real.

- The Enfield Poltergeist case inspired the 2016 horror movie "The Conjuring 2," directed by James Wan.

- One of the main criticisms of the case is that much of the evidence relies on eyewitness testimony, which is notoriously unreliable.

- Some have speculated that the girls might have been suffering from psychological issues that manifested as the poltergeist phenomena.

- Over 30 people claimed to have witnessed the strange happenings at the Hodgson's house, including neighbors, psychic researchers, and journalists.

- Although the events allegedly included furniture moving and objects flying through the air, no one was seriously injured by the poltergeist.

- At one point during the phenomena, a local priest was called to bless the house.

- The Hodgson family lived in the house until Peggy Hodgson, the mother, died in 2003. The next tenant also reported strange occurrences but was skeptical of a haunting.

- Janet claimed that during the possession episodes, she felt like she was being used by the entity to communicate, saying it felt like a "breeze" going through her.
- Despite the controversies and skepticism surrounding the Enfield Poltergeist, it remains one of the most famous and intriguing cases in the study of paranormal phenomena.

Chapter 28
The Ghost of Abraham Lincoln
Examining Sightings of the 16th President's Spirit

- The White House, apart from being the residence of the current U.S. President, is also reportedly home to several ghostly residents, the most famous being Abraham Lincoln.

- Numerous eyewitnesses, including First Ladies and foreign dignitaries, have claimed to see Lincoln's ghost wandering the corridors of the White House.

- President Lincoln's ghost is most often seen in what is known as the Lincoln Bedroom, which was originally his office.

- First Lady Grace Coolidge is reported as the first person to have actually seen Lincoln's ghost. She claimed to have seen the figure of Lincoln standing at a window in the Yellow Oval Room.

- Prime Minister Winston Churchill, during a visit to the White House, reportedly encountered Lincoln's ghost. After taking a bath, he walked back into the bedroom naked, only to find Lincoln by the fireplace. Churchill reportedly said, "Good evening, Mr. President. You seem to have me at a disadvantage."

- President Theodore Roosevelt once claimed that he could feel Lincoln's presence when he was in the White House.
- During the administration of President Franklin D. Roosevelt, a number of sightings of Lincoln's ghost were reported by visiting dignitaries and White House staff members.
- Queen Wilhelmina of the Netherlands claimed that while she was staying at the White House during World War II, she heard a knock on her bedroom door in the middle of the night. When she answered, she reportedly saw Lincoln's ghost standing in the hallway.
- President Lyndon B. Johnson, during the tumult of the Civil Rights Movement, reportedly spoke to Lincoln's ghost, asking him how he handled a similarly divided nation during the Civil War.
- Eleanor Roosevelt used the Lincoln Bedroom as her study and said she would feel Lincoln's presence while working late into the night.
- Maureen Reagan, President Ronald Reagan's daughter, reported seeing a transparent figure in the same room as her, which she believed to be the ghost of Lincoln.
- The ghost of Lincoln has not only been spotted inside the White House but has also been reportedly seen outside, particularly on the grounds around the building.
- Lincoln's ghost has supposedly been seen sitting on the edge of the bed, tying his shoes.
- Lincoln's ghost is considered a friendly presence. Most who claim to have encountered him say it was not a scary experience, but rather a comforting one.
- President Harry Truman once wrote to his wife about strange knocks and unexplained noises in the White House, speculating they might be from Lincoln's ghost.
- Some paranormal investigators speculate that the high number of Lincoln sightings could be due to his violent end and the immense stress he was under during his presidency, causing a stronger than usual spiritual imprint.
- Lincoln himself was said to have a deep interest in spiritualism and the supernatural, possibly due to the untimely death of his sons Eddie and Willie.

- Some psychics and mediums claim that Lincoln's ghost is still very active and continues to be concerned about the state of the country he once led.

- A less conventional theory suggests that what people are encountering is not Lincoln's spirit, but rather a form of residual energy - an echo of the past.

- Regardless of whether the sightings are genuine, the story of Lincoln's ghost remains an enduring part of White House lore, adding to the mystique of one of America's most historic buildings.

Chapter 29
Psychic Detectives
The Strange and Fascinating World of Paranormal Crime Solving

o Psychic detectives claim to use their supernatural abilities to solve crimes, often working alongside law enforcement or private investigators.

o In the U.S., the use of psychic detectives became particularly prominent in the 1980s, with missing person cases often featuring psychic involvement.

o Notable psychic detective Dorothy Allison claimed to have assisted in over 5,000 investigations throughout her career.

o One of the most famous psychic detectives is Allison DuBois, who inspired the TV show "Medium." She claims to have used her psychic abilities to assist law enforcement agencies across the U.S.

o Despite their popularity, there's currently no scientific evidence supporting the efficacy of psychic detectives. Their contribution to crime-solving remains controversial.

o In the UK, the Association of Chief Police Officers has guidelines stating that while they do not endorse psychics, any information provided should be evaluated in the context of the case.

- Some psychic detectives claim to use a technique known as "remote viewing" to locate missing persons or discover details about a crime scene.
- Psychic detective Noreen Renier has been involved in over 600 unsolved cases and even lectured at the FBI Academy.
- The late Sylvia Browne, a well-known psychic, claimed to have worked on 115 missing person cases, though her predictions have been heavily scrutinized and proven incorrect on several occasions.
- Despite skepticism, shows featuring psychic detectives, like "Psychic Investigators" and "Sensing Murder," have achieved significant popularity.
- A study conducted by the University of Hertfordshire found that the statements made by psychic detectives appeared to be more vague and general than specific predictions.
- A psychic detective named Etta Smith was once arrested after her accurate prediction led police to believe she was involved in a crime. She was later released and won a lawsuit for false arrest.
- Some psychic detectives claim to communicate with the spirits of victims to gain insight into their cases.
- Criticism of psychic detectives often involves the "Barnum effect," where individuals believe general statements to be uniquely applicable to them.
- Some psychic detectives claim to experience physical sensations related to the crime, such as pain or emotions that the victim felt.
- Law enforcement's use of psychic detectives is rarely officially acknowledged due to controversy and skepticism around the practice.
- In several high-profile cases, psychics have been enlisted by desperate families, like in the case of Madeleine McCann's disappearance in 2007.
- Some critics argue that psychic detectives can unintentionally lead investigations astray or give false hope to victims' families.
- Psychic detective work is not officially recognized as a profession, and there are no standard qualifications or certifications required.
- Despite ongoing debate about their legitimacy, psychic detectives continue to intrigue the public, symbolizing the intersection of paranormal belief and law enforcement.

Chapter 30
The Bell of Batoche
Examining the Legend of This Mysterious Artifact

- The Bell of Batoche is a historical artifact of great significance to the Métis people in Canada, stolen in 1885 during the Battle of Batoche.

- It's named after the town of Batoche, Saskatchewan, where the last battle of the Northwest Rebellion took place.

- The bell was taken as a war trophy by Canadian soldiers from the North-West Mounted Police, ancestors of the Royal Canadian Mounted Police.

- The Bell of Batoche mysteriously disappeared in 1991 and was missing for 22 years.

- It was supposedly taken by a group calling themselves the "Métis Commandos," who claimed responsibility for its theft.

- There is some humorous controversy around the Bell of Batoche as it was stolen, found, then stolen again — proving to be a surprisingly elusive artifact.

- The bell is said to have been found in 2005, though it was not publicly displayed until 2013 due to ongoing ownership disputes.

- Rumor has it that the bell was used as a doorstop in a private home for years before its significance was recognized.

- The Bell of Batoche was ultimately returned to the Métis people in a ceremony in Batoche in July 2013.
- During its missing years, the bell was supposedly kept in a secret location and displayed to only a select few.
- The Bell of Batoche is now housed in the Saint Antoine de Padoue Church, in Batoche, the same church from which it was originally stolen.
- The history of the bell is now part of Canadian folklore, and its journey back to its original home is a significant event for the Métis community.
- It's often jokingly said that the Bell of Batoche has seen more of Canada than most Canadians!
- A replica of the bell was made during the period it was missing, and this replica is now displayed in the Royal Canadian Mounted Police Heritage Centre.
- Some locals humorously maintain that the real Bell of Batoche is still hidden somewhere, and what was returned in 2013 is just a clever fake.
- In 2019, the Canadian playwright Ken Williams released a play called "Batoche" that tells the story of the bell and its cultural significance.
- The bell was initially used to call parishioners to mass, but it now stands as a symbol of the resilience and spirit of the Métis people.
- Some believe that the Bell of Batoche carries a curse due to its tumultuous history, though this is more local folklore than established fact.
- The return of the bell has been an important step in Canada's ongoing process of reconciliation with its Indigenous peoples.
- Despite its rather small size and unassuming appearance, the Bell of Batoche is one of the most storied and symbolic artifacts in Canadian history.

Chapter 31
The Tower of London
The Haunted History of England's Most Famous Prison

o The Tower of London, officially Her Majesty's Royal Palace and Fortress of the Tower of London, is a historic castle on the north bank of the River Thames in central London.

o Built by William the Conqueror in 1078, the Tower of London has been a royal palace, prison, treasury, and even a zoo!

o Speaking of a zoo, for over 600 years, the Tower housed a royal menagerie of exotic animals, including lions, an elephant, and even a polar bear that used to fish in the Thames.

o The Tower of London is famously known for its ravens. Legend has it that if the ravens leave, the Tower and the kingdom will fall. To avoid such a dire outcome, they keep several ravens on the grounds at all times.

o There's a Yeoman Warder (more popularly known as a Beefeater) appointed as a raven master who cares for the birds. Yes, there's a guy whose actual job is to look after the ravens!

o The Tower of London is supposedly one of the most haunted places in London. If you're lucky (or unlucky, depending on your viewpoint), you might catch sight of one of the many ghosts that supposedly haunt the tower grounds, including Anne Boleyn, a wife of Henry VIII who was beheaded there.

o Another spectral resident is said to be the White Lady, who has been seen waving at groups of school children.

o The Tower of London has served as a mint, where the country's coins were made until the early 19th century. It's said that the phrase "money for old rope" originated here, from selling off bits of worn-out rope for cash.

o It's home to the Crown Jewels, which are still in use by the royal family and include the enormous Cullinan Diamond, part of the Crown Jewels. The collection is valued at between $10 to $12 billion!

o The tower's infamous reputation as a place of torture and death peaked in the 16th and 17th centuries. The phrase "sent to the Tower" didn't exactly imply a luxurious stay.

o The last prisoner to be held in the Tower of London was Rudolf Hess, Adolf Hitler's deputy, in 1941.

o The Tower has a missing crown mystery, the crown of Edward V, who disappeared, along with the crown and his brother, in the late 15th century. The princes in the tower, anyone?

o An eccentric American, Colonel Blood, attempted to steal the Crown Jewels from the tower in 1671. He was caught, but King Charles II admired his audacity so much that he pardoned him.

o There's a superstition that the Tower's White Tower was built on a sacred Druid site, and that's why it's haunted.

o In the Medieval Palace, there's a room called the Wakefield Tower where Henry VI was murdered as he knelt in prayer.

o Contrary to popular belief, only 22 executions took place within the Tower, a meager number considering its blood-soaked reputation.

o In the 13th century, King Henry III received a pet elephant as a gift, and the creature was kept at the tower, much to the amazement and bewilderment of Londoners.

o At one point, the moat around the tower was filled with beer from a nearby brewery. Talk about a royal brew!

o Guy Fawkes, infamous for the Gunpowder Plot, was taken to the Tower to be interrogated by a council of the King's advisors.

- The tower was whitewashed in the 13th century by Henry III, which is why it's known as the "White Tower."

Chapter 32

Edgar Allan Poe

Separating Fact from Fiction About This Mysterious Writer

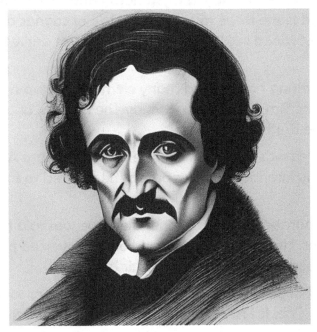

o Edgar Allan Poe was born on January 19, 1809, and is famous for his gothic and macabre writings.

o Poe is credited with writing the first modern detective story, "The Murders in the Rue Morgue," paving the way for later sleuths like Sherlock Holmes and Hercule Poirot.

o He actually didn't make much money from his writing during his lifetime. His famous poem "The Raven," for instance, earned him a meager $9, which today is equivalent to about $300. Not exactly rolling in raven feathers, was he?

o Poe was the first well-known American author to attempt to make a living strictly through writing, which in his case resulted in a financially difficult life and career.

o Edgar Allan Poe married his 13-year-old cousin, Virginia Clemm. Their relationship was much more like brother and sister than husband and wife.

o After Virginia's early death at the age of 24, Poe wrote several works about losing a beloved young woman, the most famous of these being "Annabel Lee."

o The mystery of Poe's death is a story in itself. He was found wandering the streets of Baltimore, wearing someone else's clothes, and died a few days later. The exact cause of his death remains a mystery.

o Every year on Poe's birthday, a mysterious figure known as the "Poe Toaster" would leave three roses and a bottle of cognac on Poe's grave. The tradition stopped in 2009, marking the 200th anniversary of Poe's birth.

o Poe's horror writing has inspired many elements of pop culture, including episodes of "The Simpsons," song lyrics by The Beatles, and the name of the NFL team, the Baltimore Ravens.

o Edgar Allan Poe was expelled from West Point Military Academy. This was supposedly intentional on his part as he wanted to focus on his writing career.

o Despite his reputation for dark, eerie tales, Poe was said to have a good sense of humor. He enjoyed hoaxes and once convinced people that a man had crossed the Atlantic in a hot air balloon!

o The term "Tintinnabulation," referring to the ringing or sounding of bells, was coined by Poe. It first appeared in his poem "The Bells."

o His parents were both actors, but he never knew them well. His father left the family when he was one, and his mother died from tuberculosis when he was two.

o At one point in his life, Poe was so poor that he burned his furniture to keep warm during the winter.

o Poe's cat, Catterina, was said to have sat on his shoulder while he wrote. Perhaps she was the real mastermind behind his spooky stories?

o Poe's full name is Edgar Poe. The "Allan" comes from John Allan, a merchant who took him in after his mother's death.

o Despite being known for macabre and horror, Poe considered himself primarily a poet.

o Edgar Allan Poe's image is preserved in history by the daguerreotype, an early type of photograph. One of the most famous images of him is known as the "Ultima Thule" daguerreotype.

o The Edgar Allan Poe House in Philadelphia, where Poe lived in the mid-1800s, is now a museum and National Historic Site.

o There is a talking raven named Grip in Charles Dickens' Barnaby Rudge that is said to have inspired Poe's poem "The Raven."

Chapter 33
The Winchester Mystery House
Uncovering its Strange History and Hidden

- The Winchester Mystery House is located in San Jose, California, and is known for its peculiar design, including doors and stairs that lead nowhere.

- The house was owned by Sarah Winchester, the widow of William Winchester, who made his fortune from the Winchester repeating rifle.

- According to legend, Sarah Winchester started construction on the house in 1884 because she believed she was cursed by the spirits of those killed by Winchester rifles.

- The house was under constant construction for 38 years until Sarah Winchester's death in 1922. She left no architectural plans behind.

- The Winchester Mystery House has an estimated 160 rooms, including 40 bedrooms, 2 ballrooms, 47 fireplaces, and 17 chimneys.

- Despite the large number of rooms, Sarah Winchester reportedly slept in a different room each night to confuse any malevolent spirits.

- The house's unusual features include a staircase that descends seven steps and then ascends eleven, a door that opens onto a two-story drop, and a cabinet that extends through 30 rooms of the house.

- The Winchester house also boasts a "seance room," where Sarah Winchester supposedly communicated with spirits to receive instructions on how to build the house.

- The house was constructed with an obsession for the number 13, which pops up in numerous ways - windows with 13 panes, ceilings with 13 panels, and even a staircase with 13 steps.

- The house was originally seven stories tall, but the 1906 San Francisco earthquake caused three stories to cave in. The house now stands four stories tall.

- The Winchester house is adorned with beautiful stained glass, some of which was created by the Tiffany Company.

- The property also contains gardens and outbuildings, including a fruit drying shed, a caretaker's residence, a foreman's quarters, and a garage.

- Despite her apparent fear of spirits, Sarah Winchester was a generous woman. She paid her workers well over the average daily wage and provided them with modern accommodations.

- One of the house's most peculiar features is a door that opens to a solid wall, aptly named the "Door to Nowhere."

- Sarah Winchester was very secretive about her house's construction and layout. Even her niece and personal secretary were not allowed to enter certain sections of the home.

- There's a bell on the property that was rung every night at midnight to summon the spirits and again at 2 AM to release them.

- In 2016, the Winchester Mystery House opened new rooms to the public for the first time in many years, including an attic space that contains a pump organ, Victorian couch, dress form, sewing machine and paintings.

- The Winchester Mystery House is considered one of the most haunted places in America, with reported sightings of apparitions and strange sounds.

- The house has been featured in several TV shows and movies, including an episode of Ghost Adventures and the 2018 film Winchester starring Helen Mirren as Sarah Winchester.

- Today, the Winchester Mystery House is a tourist attraction offering daily tours. Around Halloween, it also hosts flashlight tours, where visitors explore the darkened mansion with just a flashlight to guide them.

Chapter 34
The Mystery of Oak Island
Investigating its Strange and Unexplained

- Oak Island is a 140-acre island located off the coast of Nova Scotia in Canada, and it has been the center of treasure hunting activities for over two centuries.

- The story of Oak Island's treasure began in 1795 when three young boys discovered a depression in the ground that led to the famous "Money Pit."

- As the boys and eventually other treasure hunters dug deeper into the Money Pit, they found layers of logs, charcoal, coconut fiber, and putty every 10 feet, suggesting that the pit was human-made.

- At the 90-foot depth, treasure hunters reportedly found a stone with an inscribed cipher, which when translated read, "Forty feet below, two million pounds are buried."

- Despite numerous excavations and explorations, no significant treasure has been discovered on Oak Island, but various artifacts like parchment paper, a piece of gold chain, and ancient coins have been found.

- Theories about Oak Island's treasure are numerous and include pirate treasure (most famously Captain Kidd's), Marie Antoinette's lost jewels, the

Holy Grail, Shakespearean manuscripts, and even the Ark of the Covenant.

- A flood tunnel connected to the Money Pit and ending in the ocean has been a constant problem for treasure hunters. Attempts to block the flood tunnel have been unsuccessful, leading to flooding in the Money Pit and halting excavation efforts.

- Over the years, six men have died in their attempts to uncover the Oak Island treasure, leading to a legend that says seven men must die before the island will reveal its secrets.

- In the 19th century, a group known as The Oak Island Association tried to dig a new pit parallel to the Money Pit to avoid the water trap, but it ended up flooding as well.

- In 2014, the History Channel started a reality television series called "The Curse of Oak Island" about two brothers, Rick and Marty Lagina, and their efforts to find the treasure.

- The Oak Island treasure hunt is one of the longest and most expensive treasure hunts in history, costing millions of dollars and more than 200 years of continuous searching.

- In 1965, a fragment of a stone with strange symbols was found, which some have theorized is a clue to the treasure's location.

- In the late 1960s, American businessman and treasure hunter Dan Blankenship moved to Oak Island and started full-time exploration, even living on the island.

- Coconut fiber found at the Money Pit is particularly strange because coconut trees are not native to Canada, suggesting that whoever built the pit had contact with more tropical locales.

- Oak Island is now owned by Oak Island Tours, which was started by the Lagina brothers. They offer tours of the island from June to October.

- Some skeptics believe that the Oak Island mystery is a result of "confirmation bias," where people interpret information to confirm their preexisting beliefs about the treasure.

- The Money Pit's elaborate design, including its flood tunnel and booby traps, suggest that whoever buried the treasure had considerable resources and engineering knowledge.

- Over the centuries, the island has attracted a variety of famous treasure hunters, including former U.S. President Franklin D. Roosevelt, who was fascinated with the island and invested in a treasure hunt there in the early 1900s.

o In 2021, explorers found a 500-year-old crossbow bolt on the island, adding to the mystery and excitement of the treasure hunt.

o Despite the danger and uncertainty, the treasure hunt continues on Oak Island, as many are still fascinated by the mystery and the prospect of finding a hidden treasure.

Chapter 35
The Philadelphia Experiment
Investigating the Alleged Naval Experiment

- The Philadelphia Experiment is a reputed naval military experiment that is said to have occurred at the Philadelphia Naval Shipyard in Pennsylvania, USA, around October 28, 1943.

- The primary source of the story comes from a man named Carl Allen, who wrote detailed letters about the experiment under the alias "Carlos Allende."

- According to the story, the U.S. Navy destroyer escort USS Eldridge was allegedly made invisible or "cloaked" to radar detection and even the naked eye.

- The account suggests that the experiment was based on an aspect of the unified field theory, a term coined by Albert Einstein. The theory aims to describe mathematically and physically the interrelated nature of the forces that comprise electromagnetic radiation and gravity.

- The term "Philadelphia Experiment" was not used until decades after the alleged event, first appearing in the late 1950s and early 1960s.

- The story alleges that the experiment went terribly wrong. When the ship reappeared, some sailors were fused to the metal structures of the ship, including decks and bulkheads. Others supposedly went insane, and some disappeared entirely.

- Many conspiracy theorists believe the experiment was an early attempt at developing technology that could render ships invisible to radar—a feat that, if achieved, would have been of immense military value during World War II.

- The Office of Naval Research (ONR) has stated that the use of force fields to make a ship and its crew invisible does not conform to known physical laws.

- Alfred Bielek, a man who claimed to have been a part of the experiment, insisted that it was real. He said that the experiment actually involved time travel, and he had been transported to the year 2137 and later to 2749.

- Bielek's story was widely shared in some conspiracy theory circles, but his claims have been thoroughly debunked by skeptics and lack supporting evidence.

- In 1994, Jacques Vallée published an analysis of the Carlos Allende/Carl Allen annotations in the Varo Edition (a special edition of Morris K. Jessup's book) and proved that Allende/Allen had fabricated the annotations himself.

- In response to persistent requests, the U.S. Navy has stated that no such experiment occurred and that the details of the story contradict well-established physical laws.

- The USS Eldridge, the ship at the center of the story, had a rather unremarkable career during and after World War II, providing no evidence of any extraordinary events.

- The Philadelphia Experiment has inspired several books, TV shows, and films, including a 1984 science fiction movie named after the event.

- Despite a lack of credible evidence, the Philadelphia Experiment remains one of the most enduring military conspiracy theories.

- The U.S. Navy maintains that declassified materials contain no evidence of any attempts to render any ship invisible to radar or human observers.

- The story of the Philadelphia Experiment often circulates in tandem with stories of government experiments at Montauk, Long Island (known as the Montauk Project), another location with enduring tales of time travel and mind control experiments.

- Some conspiracy theorists believe that Einstein was involved in the Philadelphia Experiment, but records show that Einstein was serving as a consultant for the Navy on unrelated projects dealing with explosives and detonation during the time of the alleged experiment.

- Carl Allen/Carlos Allende, the man who initiated the story, was examined by a psychologist who diagnosed him with paranoid schizophrenia.

- The Philadelphia Experiment serves as a fascinating case study of how conspiracy theories can captivate the public imagination, despite being debunked.

Chapter 36
The Lost City of Atlantis
Separating Fact from Fiction

- The legend of Atlantis originates from ancient Greek philosopher Plato, who wrote about a beautiful technologically advanced city that sank into the sea.

- Plato described Atlantis in his dialogues "Timaeus" and "Critias," written about 360 B.C.

- According to Plato, Atlantis was a powerful and advanced kingdom that existed about 9,000 years before his own time and conquered much of Europe and Africa in prehistoric times.

- Plato described Atlantis as larger than Asia and Libya combined, located in the Atlantic just beyond the "Pillars of Hercules" — what we now call the Strait of Gibraltar.

- The fall of Atlantis, as per Plato, was the direct result of its citizens losing their virtue and moral fiber. Angering the gods with their decadence, they brought about their own downfall.

- There is a theory that the tale of Atlantis was Plato's allegory for the hubris of nations, a moral tale rather than a historical account.

- Despite extensive historical and archaeological research, there is no empirical evidence of Atlantis existing.

- Atlantis has captured imaginations for centuries, inspiring books, movies, and even the name of an American space shuttle.

- Some people have connected Atlantis with other historical events or locations, like the destruction of Thera in an enormous volcanic eruption.

- The Bahamas' Bimini Road, a submerged rock formation, has also been suggested as a possible location for Atlantis, despite geologists' explanation that it is a natural phenomenon.

- The idea of Atlantis has had a considerable impact on literature. The first notable Atlantean-inspired fiction was published in the 1880s, launching a whole genre of Atlantis-themed stories and novels.

- Some pseudoscientific theories connect the lost city of Atlantis with ancient aliens who used the city as a base for their operations on Earth.

- Edgar Cayce, a famous 20th-century psychic, made many predictions about the future discovery of Atlantis, none of which have come true to date.

- There have been countless theories about the exact location of Atlantis, with proposed sites ranging from the Mediterranean Sea to the Caribbean Sea, from the Azores islands to South America, and even Antarctica.

- Some theorists believe that Atlantis may have been an early civilization that developed advanced technology, possibly even harnessing crystal power for energy.

- Despite its lack of historical corroboration, the story of Atlantis is a cultural touchstone for the concept of advanced prehistoric lost civilizations.

- Some people associate Atlantis with the concept of 'Lemuria' or 'Mu,' hypothetical lost lands located in either the Atlantic or Indian Oceans.

- Besides the Bimini Road, other underwater structures have been associated with Atlantis, including the underwater rock formations off the coast of Japan near Yonaguni.

- A common humorous note is that Atlantis is "found" every few years by tabloid newspapers, with headlines dramatically announcing its latest discovery in a new and often improbable location.

- As of today, the lost city of Atlantis remains lost. Whether it's a real place, an allegory, or a myth, it continues to intrigue people worldwide, underlining our fascination with the idea of lost civilizations and the rise and fall of societies.

Chapter 37

The Haunted Doll Island of Mexico

The Dark Legend Behind This Eerie Place

- The "Island of the Dolls" ("La Isla de las Muñecas") is located in the Xochimilco neighborhood of Mexico City, known for its expansive system of canals and artificial islands, or chinampas.

- The island was allegedly created by a man named Julián Santana Barrera, a hermit who lived alone on this island for more than 50 years.

- According to local lore, Santana Barrera found a little girl drowned in mysterious circumstances and then saw a floating doll near the canals. He hung the doll on a tree to please the girl's spirit.

- To protect himself from the spirit and to soothe her, Santana Barrera continued to hang more dolls around the island. Eventually, he amassed hundreds of dolls—many of them in various states of decay—around the island.

- The Island of the Dolls is one of the main tourist attractions in the canal area of Xochimilco, but it's not for the faint of heart.

- Many visitors and locals believe that the dolls are possessed, with some swearing they've seen the dolls move their limbs or open their eyes.

- It's often said that the dolls whisper to each other, and some even report hearing the dolls whispering to them.

- Julián Santana Barrera died in 2001 of a heart attack. Some local legends suggest he was found drowned in the same spot where the little girl died.

- The island has appeared on many TV shows and internet series about hauntings and paranormal phenomena, adding to its spooky reputation.

- Some people leave offerings or gifts for the dolls, believing it will bring them good luck or protection from evil spirits.

- Today, the island is run by Santana Barrera's family, who charge a small entrance fee for visitors coming to see the eerie spectacle.

- Despite the eeriness of the island, it has become an increasingly popular tourist destination, attracting those with an interest in the macabre.

- You'll find all types of dolls on the Island of the Dolls, from small figurines to life-sized dolls. Some are whole, while others are decapitated, body-less, or just doll heads.

- Many of the dolls are significantly decayed or covered in dirt, adding an extra layer of creepiness to the already unsettling scene.

- Some visitors to the island claim they've felt the dolls' eyes following them. Others say they've heard the dolls whispering to each other or calling their names.

- The Island of the Dolls has been featured in several TV shows, including "Destination Truth" and "Ghost Adventures," further cementing its status as a genuinely creepy place.

- There's even a dark humor aspect to this place, with tourists often posing with the dolls for light-hearted, if somewhat macabre, selfies.

- The Island of the Dolls has inspired many horror stories and urban legends. Some say that the dolls come alive at night, moving around the island.

- It's said that the island is haunted not just by the spirit of the little girl, but also by the spirit of Santana Barrera himself, who is believed to be trapped on the island, forever hanging dolls.

- Despite its eerie reputation, the Island of the Dolls remains a unique reminder of a man's unusual dedication to the spirit of a drowned child, making it a compelling stop for any visitor to Mexico City who appreciates the more unusual aspects of local folklore.

Chapter 38
The Mary Celeste
Examining the Mysterious Disappearance of This Vessel

- The Mary Celeste was a brigantine merchant ship famously found adrift and deserted in the Atlantic Ocean, off the Azores Islands, on December 4, 1872. The ship was in a seaworthy condition, with ample provisions, but the crew was nowhere to be found.

- The last entry in the ship's log, made ten days before she was found, showed no sign of trouble and reported her last known position, near an island a few hundred miles from where she was eventually discovered.

- The vessel set sail from New York City on November 7, 1872, destined for Genoa, Italy. She was laden with 1,701 barrels of commercial alcohol intended for fortifying wines.

- The crew consisted of Captain Benjamin Briggs, his wife Sarah, their two-year-old daughter Sophia, and seven crewmen. None of them were ever seen or heard from again.

- Numerous theories have been proposed to explain the crew's disappearance: mutiny, piracy, seaquake, water spout, underwater volcanic activity, and even alien abduction!

- The ship's cargo of alcohol was not a particularly valuable one, making piracy an unlikely explanation. Also, all the barrels were found intact, except for one.

- The lifeboat was missing from the ship, which suggests that the crew had abandoned the ship for some reason, possibly fearing it was going to sink. However, why they would do so when the ship was in good condition remains a mystery.

- An inspection of the ship revealed that water in the bilge was at a level of 3.5 feet, a relatively normal amount, suggesting that the ship wasn't in danger of sinking when abandoned.

- There are some who theorize that an explosion might have scared the crew into the lifeboat. But this theory is highly speculative, and there's no solid evidence to support it.

- Arthur Conan Doyle, creator of Sherlock Holmes, wrote a fictionalized account of the mystery, "J. Habakuk Jephson's Statement," in 1884. In it, he proposed a racially charged mutiny as the cause, which sparked public interest in the case.

- When found, the ship's only lifeboat was missing and the chronometer and sextant were not on board, perhaps indicating that the captain and crew left in a hurry but planned to navigate elsewhere.

- One popular theory involves "seaquake," an underwater earthquake that could have frightened the crew into the lifeboat, only to be swallowed by the sea.

- No one was ever charged with a crime related to the disappearance of the crew, though suspicion followed the Dei Gratia (the ship that discovered the Mary Celeste) crew due to their share in salvage rights.

- One humorous suggestion is that the crew drank the alcohol cargo and mutinied or fell overboard. However, the cargo was methanol, which is not fit for consumption.

- Despite the mystery, the Mary Celeste continued to be a working ship after her crew's disappearance, changing hands several times before her last owner intentionally wrecked her in 1885 as part of an attempted insurance fraud.

- The Mary Celeste has been the subject of various works in literature and film, often embellishing the story or promoting a pet theory about the crew's disappearance.

- In 2007, an investigation by a team from the University of Michigan suggested that the Mary Celeste might have experienced a "seaquake," or earthquake at sea, which frightened the crew into abandoning ship.

- The papers of the Attorney General of Gibraltar at the time, Frederick Solly-Flood, reveal that he suspected foul play and made allegations of a conspiracy and fraud, but he was unable to prove anything.
- Interestingly, Captain Briggs was known to be a staunch abstainer from alcohol, reducing the likelihood of drunken misconduct contributing to the ship's fate.
- To this day, the fate of the Mary Celeste's crew remains one of the world's most enduring maritime mysteries, offering a haunting tale of the sea's unpredictable nature and the perils faced by those who brave her waters.

Chapter 39
King Tut
The Strange Deaths and Bad Luck Associated with This Mummy

- King Tutankhamun, often colloquially referred to as King Tut, was an ancient Egyptian pharaoh who became ruler at the age of nine or ten and reigned for about ten years, from 1332 to 1323 BC.

- Despite his enduring fame, King Tut was a relatively minor pharaoh. His tomb, however, was packed with incredible riches, and its discovery in 1922 captivated the world.

- Tutankhamun's cause of death has been a topic of considerable debate. Modern forensics have shown he may have died from complications related to a broken leg, possibly combined with genetic defects caused by inbreeding.

o The famed "curse of the pharaohs" — said to cause illness or death to those who disturb the mummies of ancient Egypt's powerful rulers — is often associated with King Tut. It was popularized by the death of Lord Carnarvon, who funded Howard Carter's excavation of Tut's tomb and died shortly thereafter.

o King Tut's burial mask is one of the most famous artifacts from ancient Egypt. The mask is made of gold, inlaid with lapis lazuli, carnelian, quartz, obsidian, turquoise, and glass, and is a magnificent representation of the young pharaoh.

o His tomb was filled with more than 5,000 artifacts, many of them remarkably well preserved. These objects provided invaluable insight into life in ancient Egypt.

o The discovery of King Tut's nearly intact tomb was a significant archaeological achievement. Prior to this, most royal tombs discovered had been robbed and emptied of their treasures.

o King Tut's mummy was subjected to several CT scans in the early 21st century, revealing he was about 5'6" tall and had a slight overbite, a common trait in the royal line of the 18th dynasty.

o One of the most popular theories about King Tut's death involves chariot racing. Some believe he fell from his chariot during a race and suffered injuries that eventually led to his death.

o King Tut's parents were brother and sister, which may have contributed to his health issues. Studies indicate that he had a cleft palate, a clubfoot, and possibly Marfan syndrome or another genetic disorder.

o King Tut was the last of his royal family to rule during the end of the 18th Dynasty. His death marked the end of this line of pharaohs.

o Contrary to popular belief, King Tut's tomb was not completely untouched by robbers. It was entered at least twice in antiquity, though the thieves did not make off with much.

o King Tut's heart was left in his body when he was mummified, a departure from the usual practice of removing the organs. Ancient Egyptians believed the heart was the seat of a person's being and intelligence.

- Despite his short reign, King Tut is often credited with restoring traditional Egyptian religion and art, both of which had been disrupted by his father's decision to worship one god, the sun disc Aten.

- In 2005, Tutankhamun was digitally reconstructed to show what he may have looked like in life. The result? A young man with a slight build and large front teeth.

- His tomb contained a dagger made of iron from a meteorite. In ancient Egypt, iron was considered to be a material of the gods due to its celestial origin.

- After his death, King Tut was erased from history by his successors until his tomb was discovered in the 20th century. This was likely because he was the last ruler of a line that was overthrown.

- The finding of King Tut's tomb led to an Egyptomania craze in the West, influencing music, fashion, and architecture.

- Some believe King Tut was murdered, although this theory has largely been debunked by recent scientific studies. The notion of a nefarious palace conspiracy certainly adds to the intrigue surrounding the young pharaoh.

- King Tut's tomb is the most intact ever discovered in the Valley of the Kings. To this day, it continues to draw visitors from all over the world, drawn by the allure of Egypt's golden boy.

Chapter 40
The Enigma of the Nazca Lines
Examining the Mysterious Geoglyphs of Peru

- The Nazca Lines are enormous geoglyphs, or designs etched into the ground, located in the Nazca Desert in southern Peru. They were designated a UNESCO World Heritage Site in 1994.

- These intriguing lines were created between 500 BC and 500 AD by the Nazca culture. They are composed of over 800 straight lines, 300 geometric figures, and 70 animal and plant designs.

- The designs range in complexity from simple lines and geometric shapes to intricate depictions of animals and plants, such as monkeys, hummingbirds, spiders, and orchids. The largest figures stretch over 1,200 feet (370 meters) across.

- The Nazca Lines were created by removing the reddish-brown iron oxide-coated pebbles that cover the surface of the Nazca desert and revealing the light-colored earth underneath.

- The Lines can be best appreciated from the air, which has led to questions about how and why they were created, considering the Nazca people didn't have the ability to fly.

- Some theories suggest that the lines were created as pathways in religious processions, while others theorize that they were an astronomical calendar, or even a way to call upon the gods for water or fertility.
- The dry, windless, and stable climate of the Nazca Desert has helped keep the lines preserved for over 2000 years.
- Despite their ancient origins, the lines weren't widely known until the 20th century, when they were spotted by a commercial aircraft.
- Some of the straight lines run up to 30 miles, while the animal and plant designs range from 50 to 1,200 feet in length.
- One of the most famous figures is the "astronaut", a humanoid figure with what appears to be a helmet or a bubble around the head, fueling many theories related to extraterrestrial involvement.
- The purpose of the Nazca lines remains a mystery. Some researchers believe they may be related to water irrigation, as some lines lead to sources of water.
- Some scholars believe the lines were made by two or more groups of people and may not all serve the same purpose.
- The Nazca lines were made by removing a top layer of rock to reveal a lighter color underneath. This means they're technically not "drawings" but a type of "negative" image.
- While there are many theories about why the Nazca lines were created, the lack of a historical record has made it impossible to be certain.
- Preservation of the Nazca Lines is a concern. Natural weather events, human encroachment, and even a Greenpeace publicity stunt have caused damage to some glyphs.
- The Nazca Lines include more than just designs. There are also numerous spirals, trapezoids, and rectangles. What these shapes signified to the Nazca remains unknown.
- The Nazca people, who are believed to have created the lines, had no written language and left little architectural footprint, contributing to the enigma of their culture and the lines they created.
- One of the more controversial theories suggests the lines were landing strips for alien spacecraft. However, scientists generally dismiss this idea.
- In 2018, Peruvian archaeologists used drone technology to discover more than 50 new examples of these mysterious desert monuments in the

adjacent Palpa province, traced onto the earth's surface in lines almost too fine to see with the human eye.

o The Nazca Lines are an extraordinary testament to the ingenuity and creativity of an ancient culture. Their preservation allows us to marvel at this mysterious and captivating aspect of human history.

Chapter 41

The Zodiac Killer

Investigating the Unidentified Serial Killer of the 1960s and 70s

- The Zodiac Killer is a pseudonym for an unidentified serial killer who operated in Northern California during the late 1960s and early 1970s. His name was derived from a series of taunting letters sent to the press, where the killer referred to himself as "Zodiac."

- The Zodiac Killer is officially linked to five murders and two attempted murders. However, in his letters, the killer claimed responsibility for up to 37 murders.

- The Zodiac Killer's confirmed victims were young couples who were targeted while alone in secluded areas at night, as well as a lone male taxi driver.

- The Zodiac Killer sent a series of cryptic letters to newspapers including The San Francisco Chronicle, The San Francisco Examiner, and The Vallejo Times Herald. These letters included complex ciphers, only some of which have been definitively solved.

- One of the killer's most famous unsolved ciphers, known as the Z340 cipher or simply "The 340," was finally cracked in 2020 by a team of independent codebreakers, over 50 years after it was originally sent.

- The Zodiac Killer's letters were marked with a distinctive symbol: a circle overlaid with a cross, similar to the astronomical symbol for the Zodiac.

- The Zodiac Killer's identity remains unknown despite thousands of tips pouring in over the years. Numerous suspects have been considered, but none have been definitively proven to be the killer.

- The case of the Zodiac Killer has become one of the most famous unsolved mysteries in America. It has inspired numerous books, movies, and TV shows, including the 2007 film "Zodiac" directed by David Fincher.

- The Zodiac Killer's letters were filled with taunts, threats, and chilling statements. In one, he stated, "The police shall never catch me, because I have been too clever for them."

- Despite a large number of investigators dedicated to the case, and the advanced forensic technology used, the identity of the Zodiac Killer remains elusive.

- The Zodiac Killer was not the first to send taunting letters to the police, but his cryptic messages and unsolved identity have made him one of the most notorious serial killers in history.

- The original Zodiac Killer investigations focused on a handful of suspects who were cleared through fingerprint analysis, handwriting analysis, or DNA testing. Still, some investigators hold onto their original suspects.

- The last known Zodiac Killer letter arrived in 1974. It included a positive review of "The Exorcist" as "the best saterical [sic] comidy [sic]."

- The Zodiac Killer's influence can be seen in other cases where killers taunted the police or the media with letters or packages, such as the BTK Killer.

- Several people have claimed to be the Zodiac Killer, or to know the killer's identity, but none of these claims have been verified.

- One of the biggest roadblocks in the Zodiac case has been the lack of physical evidence. DNA profiling wasn't available at the time of the murders, and many potential pieces of evidence have been mishandled, lost, or destroyed over the years.

- In some of his letters, the Zodiac Killer claimed he was killing people to make them his slaves in the afterlife, an idea he said he got from "The Mikado," a Gilbert and Sullivan operetta.

- The Zodiac case has attracted numerous amateur sleuths and internet detectives, who continue to propose theories and potential suspects.

- Despite decades passing since the last confirmed Zodiac murder, the case remains open in multiple jurisdictions.
- The mystery of the Zodiac Killer continues to captivate public imagination and remains one of the greatest unsolved crimes in American history, sparking endless speculation and theories about the killer's identity.

Chapter 42
The White House
Paranormal Occurrences in the Presidential Home

- The White House is not just the home of the U.S. President, but also reportedly the home of several ghosts, the most famous of which is Abraham Lincoln. Numerous sightings of Lincoln's apparition have been reported over the years by guests and staff members.

- Abigail Adams, the wife of the second U.S. President, John Adams, is another reported apparition. She is often seen in the East Room, where she used to hang laundry.

- The White House is said to be one of the most haunted houses in America, with many claiming to have seen or felt the presence of various former presidents and historical figures.

- The British soldiers who set fire to the White House during the War of 1812 are said to have left more than just physical damage. Some claim to see spectral flames or smell phantom smoke, a grim reminder of the White House's turbulent past.

- The ghost of President Andrew Jackson is said to haunt his former bedroom in the White House, the Rose Room. Witnesses have reported hearing his hearty laughter or his irritable mutterings.

- The ghost of Willie Lincoln, son of President Abraham Lincoln, is said to have been seen by numerous White House occupants, including First Lady Eleanor Roosevelt's secretary.

- One of the most frequently sighted ghostly figures is a British redcoat soldier. Some believe this spectral figure is responsible for setting the White House on fire in 1814.

- President Thomas Jefferson isn't just on the nickel and two-dollar bill - he's also been spotted in the White House, where he's said to play his violin in the Yellow Oval Room.

- The ghost of President William Henry Harrison, who was the first president to die in office, is said to haunt the White House attic, rummaging around and moving things about.

- President Lyndon B. Johnson reportedly saw the ghost of Abraham Lincoln and spoke to him, asking for advice during the Vietnam War.

- The White House ghostly presence isn't limited to people. A spectral black cat has been spotted in the basement, disappearing just as quickly as it appears.

- During the Truman administration, a new balcony was added to the White House. Since then, a ghostly figure has been seen leaning on the railing of the balcony, looking out over the lawn.

- The ghost of Dolley Madison, wife of President James Madison, is said to protect the Rose Garden. During the Wilson administration, she reportedly appeared to gardeners who were planning to dig up her beloved garden.

- The ghost of Anna Surratt, daughter of Mary Surratt who was convicted and executed as a conspirator in the assassination of Lincoln, reportedly haunts the White House, banging on the doors and pleading for her mother's life.

- During the Coolidge administration, the first lady reportedly saw the ghost of a woman wearing a cap and a shawl, thought to be the spirit of Abigail Adams.

- The Red Room, one of three state parlors on the first floor, is said to be home to the ghost of an unidentified soldier from the War of 1812.

- Visitors and staff have reported hearing President Taft taking a bath in the early morning hours. Some claim to have heard him splashing and humming to himself.

- The demon cat, or "D.C." as it's known, is a spectral feline said to appear in the basement and crypt of the Capitol building before national tragedies, but it has also been sighted in the White House.

- The White House has served as a residence for U.S. Presidents since John Adams in 1800. With all its history and countless inhabitants, it's no wonder it's considered one of the most haunted places in the U.S.

- Some say that the ghostly presence in the White House isn't limited to just the main building. The spectral figure of a man has been reported multiple times at the North Portico, appearing to wait for something or someone before vanishing.

Chapter 43
The Legend of Sleepy Hollow
Separating Fact from Fiction About This Terrifying Tale

o The Legend of Sleepy Hollow is a gothic story written by Washington Irving and first published in 1820. It tells the tale of a superstitious schoolmaster who encounters a headless horseman.

o Sleepy Hollow is a real place. It's a village in the town of Mount Pleasant, New York.

o The Headless Horseman is said to be the ghost of a Hessian soldier who lost his head to a cannonball during the Revolutionary War.

o The protagonist, Ichabod Crane, is a schoolteacher from Connecticut who moves to Sleepy Hollow for work. His character is often portrayed as lanky and somewhat fearful.

o Brom Bones, Ichabod Crane's rival in the story, is thought to have disguised himself as the Headless Horseman to scare Ichabod away and win the heart of Katrina Van Tassel, the woman they both desire.

o The story's enduring popularity has led to countless adaptations, including a 1999 movie directed by Tim Burton and a TV series that aired from 2013 to 2017.

o The legend has made the small village of Sleepy Hollow a popular tourist destination, especially around Halloween.

- Every Halloween, the village of Sleepy Hollow hosts a festival known as the "Great Jack O'Lantern Blaze," featuring thousands of hand-carved pumpkins.
- The bridge where Ichabod Crane encounters the Headless Horseman is real. The original was located on the Albany Post Road over the Pocantico River.
- The Old Dutch Church and its adjacent Sleepy Hollow Cemetery, where the Headless Horseman is said to be buried, is still standing and open for tours.
- In the story, the Headless Horseman is said to be unable to cross bridges. This belief was widespread in European folklore where spirits and supernatural beings had this limitation.
- The character of Ichabod Crane was reportedly based on an actual schoolteacher whom Washington Irving had met in Kinderhook, New York.
- There's a bronze statue of the Headless Horseman, in pursuit of Ichabod Crane, near the Sleepy Hollow Village Hall.
- Washington Irving himself is buried in Sleepy Hollow Cemetery, along with other prominent figures like Andrew Carnegie and Walter Chrysler.
- There is a Sleepy Hollow Street in the town of Concord, Massachusetts, which is said to have been an inspiration for Irving's story.
- Washington Irving was influenced by German folktales, which feature their own headless apparitions, when writing The Legend of Sleepy Hollow.
- The character of Katrina Van Tassel is often portrayed as a coquette in adaptations of the story, but in Irving's original text, her personality is not deeply explored.
- Sleepy Hollow was initially known as North Tarrytown. It officially changed its name to Sleepy Hollow in 1996, embracing the fame of Irving's story.
- "The Legend of Sleepy Hollow" is often paired with another one of Irving's stories, "Rip Van Winkle," as two tales of supernatural happenings in the Hudson Valley.
- The tale suggests that the Headless Horseman was not a ghost but an invention of Brom Bones to win Katrina's hand by scaring away his rival, Ichabod Crane.

Chapter 44
The Salem Witch Trials
The Origins and Legacy of This Dark Period in American History

- The Salem Witch Trials took place in colonial Massachusetts between February 1692 and May 1693. It was one of the most infamous events in American history.

- More than 200 people were accused of practicing witchcraft, the Devil's magic, during the trials.

- The hysteria began when a group of young girls in Salem Village claimed to be possessed by the devil and accused several local women of witchcraft.

- As a wave of hysteria spread throughout colonial Massachusetts, a special court was convened in Salem to hear the cases.

- Nineteen of the accused, 14 women and five men, were hanged at Gallows Hill near Salem Village.

- One man, Giles Corey, was crushed to death by stones for refusing to enter a plea.

- Five others, including two infants, died in jail.

- The Salem witch trials ended when the use of spectral evidence was declared inadmissible. Spectral evidence is a form of testimony based on dreams and visions rather than hard evidence.

- The Salem Witch Trials led to the implementation of the "innocent until proven guilty" ideology in the American judicial system.

- One theory suggests the cause of the strange behavior by those claiming to be possessed was a disease brought on by eating rye bread made from grain infected with the fungus ergot, which can cause hallucinations.

- Some of the symptoms the girls displayed are similar to epilepsy, which can also cause hallucinations and physical convulsions.

- In 1953, Arthur Miller dramatized the events of 1692 in his play "The Crucible", using them as an allegory for the anti-Communist "witch hunts" led by Senator Joseph McCarthy in the 1950s.

- There are no known witches or wizards buried in the Salem Witch Trials Memorial; instead, it honors their memory and marks the injustice of their deaths.

- In 1992, to mark the 300th anniversary of the trials, the city erected the Salem Witch Trials Memorial.

- "The Witches: Salem, 1692" is a bestselling non-fiction book about the trials by Stacy Schiff.

- The "Witch House" in Salem is the only building still standing with direct ties to the witch trials. The home belonged to Judge Jonathan Corwin.

- Not all "witches" were women. About 20% of those accused and convicted during the Salem Witch Trials were men.

- Salem, now known as "The Witch City," has embraced its witchy past and present. Today, you can visit museums, attend a witch trial reenactment, or even buy a magical potion at one of the city's many witch shops.

- In 1711, the colony passed a bill restoring the rights and good names of those accused of witchcraft and granted £600 restitution to their heirs.

- The Salem witch trials were the deadliest witch hunt in the history of colonial North America.

Chapter 45
The Devil's Bible
The Mysterious Origins and Content of the Codex Gigas

- The Devil's Bible, also known as the Codex Gigas (Latin for "Giant Book"), is the largest extant medieval manuscript in the world.

- It was created in the early 13th century in the Benedictine monastery of Podlažice in Bohemia, a region in the modern-day Czech Republic.

- The Codex Gigas is famous for its full-page illustration of the Devil, leading to its nickname.

- The manuscript contains the Vulgate translation of the Christian Bible, but also includes other texts: a calendar, the "Ars medicinae" (a book on medical practices), the "Chronica Boemorum" (a history of Bohemia), and others.

- It is written in Latin and includes illuminations (decorations) that are colored red, blue, yellow, green, and gold.

- The legend surrounding the Codex Gigas says that it was written by a monk who was sentenced to be walled up alive for breaking his monastic vows. To avoid punishment, he promised to create a book that would glorify the monastery forever, and he would do it in a single night.

- According to the legend, the monk soon realized that the task was impossible, so he prayed to the devil for help, selling his soul in the process.

The devil completed the manuscript, and the monk added the devil's picture out of gratitude.

o   While it's an interesting story, it's more likely the Codex Gigas took over 20 years to complete due to its size and the detail of its calligraphy and illuminations.

o   The book is 36 inches tall, 20 inches wide, and almost 9 inches thick. It weighs about 165 pounds.

o   The Devil's portrait is the largest one in the book and it's the only image that takes up a full page.

o   During the 30 Years War in the 17th century, the Swedes took the Codex Gigas as plunder. It remains in Sweden to this day.

o   The Devil's Bible is currently kept at the National Library in Stockholm, Sweden, where it's been since 1649.

o   In 2007, National Geographic aired a documentary about the Codex Gigas called "The Devil's Bible."

o   In the Devil's picture, he is depicted in an ermine loincloth. Ermine was traditionally used in depictions of Christ, which makes this detail in the devil's depiction highly unusual.

o   Due to the Codex Gigas' size, it's believed that the book originally required two people to move.

o   The Codex Gigas was made from more than 160 animal skins. It's estimated that 600 cows would have been needed to provide enough vellum for the book.

o   The Codex was rebound in the 19th century. The book's wooden boards are covered in leather and ornate metal.

o   A digital version of the Codex Gigas, including a virtual model of the binding and the edges, is available for viewing on the website of the National Library of Sweden.

o   The mystery surrounding the Codex Gigas is not just about who wrote it, but also about the peculiar nature of its texts. Along with the Bible, there are magical formulas, a list of brothers in the Podlažice monastery, and a calendar with a necrology, magic formulas, among other texts.

o   Despite its name and the legend, the Devil's Bible does not contain satanic verses or black magic rituals.

Chapter 46

Skinwalkers

The Terrifying Navajo Legends of Shape-Shifting Witches

- A Skinwalker, in Navajo culture, is a type of harmful witch who has the ability to transform, possess, or disguise themselves as an animal.

- The Navajo term for skinwalker is "yee naaldlooshii" which translates to "he who walks on all fours."

- Stories of Skinwalkers are not just prevalent in Navajo culture, but can be found in various Indigenous tribes across North America.

- Skinwalkers are typically associated with death and destruction. They are believed to be able to cause disease and misfortune.

- Skinwalkers are known for their ability to change their shape into various types of animals, such as coyotes, wolves, foxes, cougars, dogs, and bears.

- Some stories even say that Skinwalkers can take the form of birds or can mimic the characteristics of people.

- To become a Skinwalker, it's believed that a member of the tribe must commit a tremendous social taboo, such as murder.

- Skinwalkers are often associated with disturbing events or malevolent acts due to their role as witches in Navajo culture.

- Despite being a part of Navajo tradition, discussions about Skinwalkers are generally considered taboo. It's believed that speaking about these beings can draw their attention and potentially lead to harm.

- It's thought that Skinwalkers wear the skins of the animals they transform into - hence the name.

- Skinwalkers have been said to have the power to read human thoughts or hypnotize individuals, leading them to act out of character.

- They have also been associated with the ability to control the creatures of the night and to bring forth spirits from the underworld.

- Stories of Skinwalkers are often used as a way to teach and enforce societal norms in Navajo culture, as becoming a Skinwalker is associated with the breaking of cultural taboos.

- In Navajo tradition, it's believed that the eyes of a Skinwalker glow like an animal's when they are in human form, and when in animal form, their eyes do not glow as an animal's would.

- Skinwalkers, according to lore, are not immortal, but they are difficult to kill. Traditional belief suggests that to kill a Skinwalker, one must know who the person is in their human form and speak their full name in person.

- The Skinwalker Ranch in Utah, named after the mythical creature, is a hotspot for UFO sightings, and it's also said to be cursed.

- Stories of Skinwalkers are not just part of folklore; there are people who claim to have had encounters with these beings in the present day.

- Because of the sensitive nature of Skinwalkers in Navajo culture, a lot of the knowledge about them is not shared with outsiders and remains largely a mystery to the outside world.

- Skinwalkers are also believed to be able to make themselves invisible, which allows them to spy on others without being detected.

- Despite their notoriety, Skinwalkers represent only a small fraction of what Navajo witches can potentially do, as Navajo traditional belief encompasses a broad spectrum of other witchcraft practices.

Chapter 47
The Tower of Silence
Exploring the Zoroastrian Rituals of Sky Burial

- The "Tower of Silence", also known as a Dakhma, is a circular, raised structure used by Zoroastrians for exposure of the dead.

- Zoroastrians believe that the earth and fire are sacred and should not be polluted with decaying matter. Therefore, the dead bodies are not buried or cremated but left in these towers for vultures to consume.

- The primary purpose of this process is the disposal of the dead in a manner that is considered clean and avoids polluting the earth.

- The Towers of Silence are mostly found in Iran and India, where Zoroastrian populations are concentrated.

- The interior of the tower is built with concentric rings where the bodies are placed. Men are placed in the outer circle, women in the middle, and children in the innermost circle.

- The corpses are completely stripped of flesh by the vultures within a few hours.

- After the bones have been bleached by the sun and wind, which can take as long as a year, they are collected and placed in an ossuary pit in the center of the tower.

- Traditionally, Towers of Silence are built on hilltops or on elevated terrain to keep the place isolated and away from populated areas.
- The practice of using Towers of Silence has decreased significantly due to shrinking vulture populations in areas like India, caused in part by the use of the drug Diclofenac in livestock.
- While the traditional practice is not widely used today, many Towers of Silence are preserved as heritage sites.
- Despite the morbid association, the Towers of Silence represent a significant part of Zoroastrian culture, emphasizing their beliefs in purity and the cycle of life and death.
- The design and concept of the Tower of Silence are believed to be thousands of years old and are attributed to the prophet Zoroaster himself.
- The towers are usually built with locally available stone and are remarkably durable.
- The last functioning Tower of Silence in India is located in Mumbai and is surrounded by a lush, 54-acre park, making it a jarring juxtaposition of life and death.
- To this day, there's a certain stigma and fear associated with these towers due to their function. This has led to many myths and ghost stories surrounding the Towers of Silence.
- Zoroastrians in the diaspora have had to adapt their funerary practices due to the unavailability of Towers of Silence. In many cases, they have adopted cremation or burial.
- According to Zoroastrian belief, the vultures are not just disposing of the dead; they are performing a religious rite.
- The Towers of Silence came under severe scrutiny during the British colonial rule in India, primarily due to cultural misunderstanding.
- It's considered a serious religious offence to visit the interior of a Tower of Silence if you are not a Zoroastrian corpse-bearer.
- Despite their name, the Towers of Silence are often bustling with life. The surrounding areas are usually filled with trees and frequented by various birds, making these sites an ironic hub of biodiversity.

Chapter 48
The Dyatlov Pass Incident
Examining the Mysterious Deaths of Nine Hikers in the Ural Mountains

o The Dyatlov Pass Incident refers to the mysterious deaths of nine skilled hikers in the northern Ural Mountains of Russia on February 2, 1959.

o The group, led by Igor Dyatlov, was comprised of seven men and two women, all students or graduates of Ural Polytechnical Institute.

o The incident took place during a difficult trek that was expected to cover 300 km. The route was classified as "Category III," the most challenging.

o All nine bodies were found in odd circumstances. They had abandoned their tent, which had been cut open from the inside, and fled to the woods without proper clothing despite the sub-zero temperatures.

o Six members of the group died of hypothermia, while three others showed signs of physical trauma, including fractured skulls and chest injuries.

o One of the female hikers was missing her tongue, eyes, part of the lips, as well as facial tissue and a fragment of skull bone.

o Soviet investigators determined that an "unknown compelling force" had caused the deaths. The incident's files were sent to a secret archive, and the case was abandoned due to the absence of a guilty party.

- Numerous theories have been put forward to explain the incident. These include everything from an avalanche to secret military tests, infrasound-induced panic, and even encounters with extraterrestrial life.

- The last photo on one of the hiker's cameras shows a mysterious glowing object, fueling speculations about UFOs.

- The campsite was made on the slope of Kholat Syakhl, which translates to "Dead Mountain" in the local indigenous Mansi language.

- Despite the investigation's official closure in 1959, interest in the Dyatlov Pass Incident persisted, and the area became a popular spot for adventure tourism in Russia.

- It wasn't until 2019 that Russian authorities reopened an investigation into the incident. However, the new investigation only considered natural explanations, ruling out theories involving military testing or extraterrestrial involvement.

- The tent, found half torn down and covered with snow, contained all the group's belongings, including shoes and outerwear, suggesting a sudden and frantic departure.

- Footprints leading away from the tent toward the woods were visible, but they abruptly stopped about 500 meters away.

- Autopsies showed that all of the hikers had died 6 to 8 hours after their last meal, and traces of alcohol were found in their bodies.

- One of the investigators reported that the victims' clothing contained a high level of radioactive contamination.

- Despite the sub-zero temperatures, some of the victims were found wearing only underwear. This behavior is consistent with "paradoxical undressing," a known behavior of hypothermia victims when they start to feel a burning sensation and undress.

- In 2020, the Russian Prosecutor General's office concluded that an avalanche was the most likely cause of the tragedy. However, this explanation remains controversial, with critics pointing out inconsistencies and lack of evidence.

- The Dyatlov Pass Incident has been the inspiration for numerous books, movies, and video games, each offering their own interpretation of the event.

- The pass where the incident occurred was named Dyatlov Pass in honor of the group's leader, Igor Dyatlov.

Chapter 49
The Shadow People
Investigating Reports of Dark Entities Lurking in the Night

o Shadow people, also known as shadow figures, shadow beings, or black masses, are the perception of a patch of shadow as a living, humanoid figure, particularly as interpreted by believers in the paranormal or supernatural.

o These entities are often reported moving with quick, jerky movements, and quickly disintegrate or move through walls when noticed.

o They are usually reported to be humanoid figures seen in the viewer's peripheral vision, appearing to dart behind furniture or walls, or stand at the end of the bed.

o The term "shadow people" was popularized by author and paranormal investigator Heidi Hollis, who describes them as dark silhouettes with human shapes and profiles.

o Hollis believes shadow people have malicious intentions and are different from ghost sightings because they're often seen straight on instead of peripherally.

o Shadow people are frequently reported to behave in a manner that suggests a malevolent intent to harm or induce fear in the observer.

o Some experiencers report a feeling of dread associated with the appearance of shadow beings, and many claim to also feel other sensations, such as cold spots or a static electric feeling.

- Many theories have been proposed to explain the phenomenon of shadow people. These range from time-traveling humans and interdimensional beings to demons or spirits.

- In some cases, shadow people have been linked to sleep paralysis, a condition where an individual wakes up unable to move, often accompanied by hallucinations of ominous figures.

- The phenomenon is frequently reported in association with episodes of sleep deprivation and over-exhaustion.

- Certain drugs, particularly stimulants like methamphetamine, have been associated with an increased likelihood of experiencing shadow people.

- In the realm of the paranormal, some have suggested that shadow people could be the manifestation of a spirit or entity that is trying to gather enough energy to fully materialize.

- Some cultures interpret these figures as the presence of entities or spirits from other realms, or even as omens of death.

- Paranormal investigators and enthusiasts use a variety of tools, including EMF meters, infrared cameras, and digital voice recorders, in an attempt to gather evidence of shadow people.

- Some people have reported shadow people wearing a hat or a hood, and these specific entities are often referred to as the "Hat Man" or the "Hooded Shadow."

- There have been numerous accounts of shadow people encounters throughout history, with similar descriptions appearing in folklore and ghost stories worldwide.

- Shadow people have become a popular subject in horror and science fiction media, appearing in films, video games, and literature.

- While shadow people are largely a modern phenomenon, similar supernatural entities have been reported in cultures throughout history, including shadowy spiritual beings in various religious traditions.

- Psychologists and neuroscientists have proposed that seeing shadow figures could be a form of pareidolia - the tendency to interpret vague or random images as something meaningful.

- Despite the lack of empirical evidence, belief in shadow people remains widespread, contributing to a growing body of stories, experiences, and speculations about these eerie apparitions.

Chapter 50
The Bellamy Bridge Ghost
Uncovering the Legend of Florida's Most Haunted Bridge

- The Bellamy Bridge is an historic site in Marianna, Florida. It is one of the oldest metal bridges in Florida, built in 1914.

- The bridge and surrounding area are famous for a local legend about the ghost of Elizabeth Jane Bellamy, who is said to haunt the vicinity.

- According to local folklore, Elizabeth died tragically on her wedding night in 1837, when her wedding dress caught fire.

- Legend claims that her spirit was unable to find peace and has been seen as a spectral lady in white, haunting the old bridge and surrounding swamp ever since.

- Multiple versions of the Bellamy Bridge ghost story exist, but they all agree on the fiery death of a young bride and her subsequent haunting of the area.

- Elizabeth's ghost is often reported floating over the waters of the Chipola River or disappearing among the trees of the swampy surroundings.

- The tales have become so popular that the area around the bridge has been officially named the "Bellamy Bridge Heritage Trail" and includes a "Ghost Walk".

- Many visitors have reported unexplained phenomena such as orbs, mists, and even ghostly apparitions in photographs taken at the site.
- Elizabeth's ghost has also been associated with other eerie phenomena like strange lights, disembodied voices, and feelings of unexplained dread.
- Some versions of the legend say that her husband, Dr. Samuel Bellamy, died of a broken heart shortly after Elizabeth's death and also haunts the area.
- Interestingly, historical records show that Elizabeth actually died of malaria, not from a fire. However, the fiery death version makes for a more dramatic story and has stuck in local folklore.
- The Bellamy Bridge Ghost is one of Florida's oldest ghost stories and has been told and retold in various forms for over a century.
- Despite the real causes of death, many believe in the ghostly sightings and the area continues to attract ghost hunters and paranormal enthusiasts.
- The Bellamy Bridge is a frequent location for local ghost tours and paranormal investigations, especially around Halloween.
- Several books and documentaries have featured the Bellamy Bridge ghost story, contributing to its reputation as one of Florida's most haunted locations.
- Even skeptics who have visited the area have reported feeling an eerie presence or chill in the air, contributing to the bridge's haunted reputation.
- The legend of the Bellamy Bridge Ghost has played a significant role in shaping local culture and history, and the story continues to be passed down through generations.
- Some visitors to the site have reported seeing other ghostly figures near the bridge, suggesting that Elizabeth may not be the only spirit haunting the area.
- Interestingly, the actual bridge is the third to stand in the location. The original wooden bridge, where the haunting is said to have started, burned down many years ago.
- Whether fact or fiction, the story of the Bellamy Bridge Ghost has become a defining element of the local area, demonstrating the enduring power of folklore and ghost stories.

Chapter 51
The Winchester Geese
The Tragic History of London's Medieval Brothels

- ○ The Winchester Geese is a term that was historically used to refer to the prostitutes who worked in the Southwark area of London during the 12th to 17th centuries.

- ○ These women were called "Winchester Geese" because they operated within the Liberty of the Bishop of Winchester, an area outside of the jurisdiction of the City of London.

- ○ Despite being in charge of the area, the Bishop of Winchester was famously hypocritical, profiting from the brothels while publicly condemning the women's immoral actions.

- ○ The area of Southwark, known as The Bankside, was known for its brothels, theatres, bear pits, and other forms of entertainment that were considered immoral by the standards of the time.

- ○ The term "Winchester Geese" has since come to be associated with the women buried in Crossbones Graveyard, an unmarked mass grave discovered during construction in Southwark in 1992.

- ○ The graveyard is thought to hold the remains of approximately 15,000 people, many of whom were presumably Winchester Geese, and was in use from the medieval period until 1853.

- ○ Today, the site of Crossbones Graveyard has become a place of remembrance and pilgrimage, with visitors leaving tokens of respect and memory tied to the gates.

- Many versions of the story of the Winchester Geese contain elements of the supernatural, with stories of ghostly figures seen at Crossbones Graveyard and around Southwark.
- There's a longstanding tradition of a Halloween procession that ends at the gates of Crossbones Graveyard in remembrance of the Winchester Geese.
- The stories of the Winchester Geese have served as the inspiration for several novels, plays, and pieces of artwork, attesting to their lasting cultural impact.
- The term "Goose" in this context was used as a derogatory term for prostitutes, referencing the slang term "goosing" for sexual activity.
- The Winchester Geese were often social outcasts in life, as prostitution was seen as immoral. However, they were integral to the economic success of Southwark.
- There's an urban legend that the Bishop of Winchester would regularly walk through the brothels, not for pleasure, but to collect his fees.
- The women who were the Winchester Geese had their own rules and system of governance, demonstrating a significant level of independence and control over their profession.
- Every year on the 23rd of November, a memorial ceremony known as the "Outcast Dead Rites" is held at the Crossbones Graveyard in honor of the Winchester Geese.
- The stories of the Winchester Geese often blur the line between history and myth, with some of the more salacious details likely being embellishments or outright fabrications.
- In 2006, a memorial plaque was installed at Crossbones Graveyard to commemorate the Winchester Geese and all those who were buried there.
- Despite the historical stigma attached to them, the Winchester Geese have become symbols of women's history, social history, and the history of sex work in London.
- Archaeological excavations at the site of Crossbones Graveyard have revealed insights into the lives and deaths of the Winchester Geese.
- The legacy of the Winchester Geese continues to inspire discussions about the decriminalization and destigmatization of sex work today.

Chapter 52

The Beast of Bray Road

The Wisconsin Legend of a Werewolf-Like Creature

- The Beast of Bray Road is a cryptid, or unknown creature, reported to have been seen in Elkhorn, Wisconsin, primarily during the late 1980s and early 1990s.

- It's typically described as a large, hairy creature on all fours, but with the ability to stand on two legs, much like a werewolf.

- Witnesses often compare the Beast of Bray Road to a bear or big wolf, although its upright posture and humanoid characteristics distinguish it from common wildlife.

- Bray Road, the site of the creature's alleged sightings, is a rural road on the outskirts of Elkhorn, hence the creature's name.

- Linda Godfrey, a local reporter, is credited with bringing the Beast of Bray Road to widespread public attention. Her initial article led to a book and multiple TV documentary appearances.

- Godfrey collected dozens of sighting reports, which she claims were credible and sincere. These encounters usually involved the creature seen on or near the road, often at night.

- Some local theories posit that the Beast of Bray Road is a spiritual entity or a creature from Native American folklore.

- Other theories suggest the beast could be a cryptid known as a Dogman, a creature reported in various parts of North America and bearing similarities to the descriptions of the Beast of Bray Road.

- Despite numerous sightings, no physical evidence like fur or footprints has ever been definitively linked to the Beast of Bray Road.

- The Beast of Bray Road became the subject of the 2005 horror movie "The Beast of Bray Road," which portrayed the creature as a werewolf-like entity.

- The creature is sometimes linked to other mysterious phenomena in the area, such as unexplained livestock deaths and disappearances.

- Skeptics often attribute the Beast of Bray Road sightings to misidentified wildlife, hoaxes, or the result of fear and imagination.

- The sightings sparked a minor tourism boost in the Elkhorn area, with some local businesses capitalizing on the interest in the Beast of Bray Road.

- In popular culture, the Beast of Bray Road is often depicted similarly to a classic werewolf, complete with a menacing posture and a fearsome howl.

- Some sightings describe the beast with glowing or reflective eyes, a common feature in many cryptid reports.

- While the frequency of reported sightings has decreased since the 1990s, the Beast of Bray Road remains a popular subject of cryptid enthusiasts.

- Some witnesses claim that the creature has displayed aggressive behavior, such as chasing cars, but no physical attacks on humans have been reported.

- Despite its fearsome reputation, there are also reports of the beast appearing indifferent to human observers, contributing to its enigmatic nature.

- The creature has been featured in various TV shows, podcasts, and web series discussing cryptids, paranormal events, and unexplained mysteries.

- Despite more than three decades since the initial reports, the Beast of Bray Road continues to be a subject of fascination, speculation, and debate.

Chapter 53
The Axeman of New Orleans
The Mysterious Serial Killer Who Preyed on Italian Immigrants

- The Axeman of New Orleans was a serial killer who operated in New Orleans and surrounding communities from May 1918 to October 1919.

- The Axeman gained his name due to his brutal modus operandi: he would break into homes and attack his victims with an axe or a straight razor.

- Interestingly, the Axeman often used tools found within the victims' homes for the attacks, instead of bringing his own.

- The Axeman's victims were typically Italian or Italian-American, leading to speculation that the crimes might have been ethnically motivated.

- The Axeman created a wave of panic throughout New Orleans, leading residents to secure their homes and police to increase their patrols.

- In March 1919, a letter was published in local newspapers purportedly from the Axeman, wherein he claimed to be a demon from Hell and offered to spare anyone who played jazz music in their homes.

- This infamous letter led to a city-wide frenzy of jazz music playing on the night the Axeman had designated in his letter.

- No attacks were reported on that jazz-filled night, adding to the Axeman's terrifying mystique.

- Despite intense police investigations and public anxiety, the Axeman was never identified or apprehended.

- The crimes stopped as abruptly as they started, with no clear reason why they ended.

- In total, the Axeman is believed to have killed six people and injured another six, though some believe he may have had other unknown victims.

- The Axeman's story has been featured in many books, podcasts, and TV shows about unsolved crimes and historical mysteries.

- The case of the Axeman was notably included in the TV show "American Horror Story: Coven," with actor Danny Huston playing the title role.

- Several theories about the Axeman's identity and motivations have been proposed, but none have been conclusively proven.

- Some theories suggest that the Axeman was involved in organized crime, while others posit that he might have been a disturbed individual with a personal grudge.

- Despite the reign of terror, some reports suggested that New Orleans citizens began to carry axes as a form of protection against the Axeman.

- The Axeman of New Orleans has become a part of New Orleans folklore, and his story is often included in local ghost tours.

- The Axeman's infamous letter has been the subject of numerous analyses, with some arguing it might have been a hoax by a local journalist.

- The Axeman's story has been cited as an early example of a media-driven frenzy around a serial killer.

- Over a century later, the case of the Axeman of New Orleans remains one of America's most infamous unsolved mysteries.

Chapter 54
The Black Monk of Pontefract
The Haunting of One of England's Most Terrifying Houses

- The Black Monk of Pontefract, also known as the "Pontefract Poltergeist," is one of the most notorious reported hauntings in the UK.

- The haunting took place at 30 East Drive in Pontefract, West Yorkshire, and began in the 1960s.

- The Pritchard family, who lived in the house, reported a wide variety of phenomena, including objects moving on their own, green foam appearing from taps and toilets, and mysterious black cloaked figures.

- The entity was dubbed the "Black Monk" due to the belief that it was the spirit of a Cluniac monk who was hanged in the area for the crime of rape and murder during the 16th century.

- This monastic figure was reportedly seen numerous times, wearing a black robe with a hood that obscured his face.

- The family's daughter, Diane, was supposedly the focus of the haunting, with reports of her being dragged up the stairs by an invisible hand and mysterious scratches appearing on her body.

- Despite the frightening phenomena, the Pritchard family chose to continue living at 30 East Drive for several years.

- Even after the Pritchards moved out, subsequent residents and visitors have reported paranormal activity in the house.

- The house at 30 East Drive remains a popular destination for paranormal investigators and has been featured on numerous television shows and documentaries about hauntings.

- A film, "When The Lights Went Out," was released in 2012, which was based on the alleged haunting and the experiences of the Pritchard family.

- It is often reported that the haunting was so severe it culminated in the levitation of Diane Pritchard, a story that is widely known in paranormal circles.

- The Black Monk was also known to be quite the prankster. The family recounted instances of milk being poured out onto the kitchen floor and buttons being popped off television sets.

- One of the creepier aspects of the case was the "cold spots" which would appear around the house, particularly on the staircase and in Diane's bedroom.

- The entity was also known to turn lights on and off, leading to the film's title, "When The Lights Went Out."

- Visitors to the house today often leave religious artefacts in an attempt to cleanse the house of its supposed dark presence.

- It has been reported that no one has ever lasted more than four days while staying at 30 East Drive.

- Despite the fearsome reputation, the house was put up for rent for those daring enough to spend the night.

- Regular vigils are held at the house by ghost hunters, with many reporting sudden drops in temperature and mysterious apparitions.

- The house still retains its 1960s decor to maintain the authenticity of the period when the haunting took place.

- Over half a century later, the story of the Black Monk of Pontefract continues to fascinate and terrify those interested in the paranormal.

Chapter 55
The Catacombs of Paris
The Dark Tunnels Beneath the City of Light

- The Catacombs of Paris, also known as "Les Catacombes," are an underground ossuary holding the remains of over six million people.

- They were created in the late 18th century as a response to the overcrowding of Parisian cemeteries.

- The Catacombs consist of a network of old cave systems and tunnels from ancient limestone quarries spanning roughly 200 miles beneath the city streets.

- The name "Catacombs" was used during the Romantic Era and was a direct reference to the Roman catacombs, which had fascinated the public since their discovery.

- The walls of the Catacombs are arranged with bones and skulls in various decorative patterns, creating a macabre artistry.

- The entrance to the Catacombs is marked with a chilling inscription: "Stop, this is the empire of death."

- Despite the vast network of tunnels, only a small part of the Catacombs (about 1.2 miles) is open to the public.

- In the past, the Catacombs have been used for various activities, including secret concerts, clandestine meetings, and even illegal parties known as "cataphiles."
- During World War II, the French Resistance used parts of the Catacombs to hide from German troops.
- The Catacombs have been featured in numerous films and literature, enhancing their eerie reputation.
- Some people report feeling a strange energy or experiencing unexplained phenomena when exploring the Catacombs, leading to claims of paranormal activity.
- The constant temperature in the Catacombs is around 14°C (57°F), making it a cold experience, regardless of the weather above ground.
- It takes about 45 minutes to tour the public section of the Catacombs. Make sure to wear good walking shoes as there are around 130 steps down and then another 83 back up.
- It is illegal to enter the Catacombs after hours, and those caught can face heavy fines.
- The Catacombs have been meticulously mapped and explored, but legends persist of people who have gotten lost and never been found.
- The Philosopher's stone, the legendary alchemical substance, was reputedly found in the Catacombs of Paris by Nicolas Flamel.
- Many famous people's remains lie in the Catacombs, including Charles Perrault, author of "Cinderella," "Little Red Riding Hood," and other classic fairy tales.
- The Catacombs house a Sepulchral Lamp, which burned indefinitely in the past. It was kept alight by the gases emanating from the decomposing bodies.
- The last door in the Catacombs reads: "In the peace of the shadows, they sleep the eternal sleep."
- The Catacombs are deemed a macabre tourist attraction and a vital piece of Paris's history and heritage.

Chapter 56
The Dancing Plague of 1518
The Bizarre Mass Hysteria That Swept Through Strasbourg

o The Dancing Plague of 1518 is one of the most bizarre and unexplained events in human history. It began in July 1518 in the city of Strasbourg, which is now located in modern-day France.

o The "dancing" epidemic started when a woman named Frau Troffea started dancing fervently in a street in Strasbourg.

o Frau Troffea danced relentlessly for days, and within a week, 34 others had joined her, and by the end of the month, the dancing epidemic had spread to around 400 people.

o The dancing was not merry or recreational; instead, it was frantic, ceaseless, and often resulted in injury or death.

o People were literally dancing themselves to death, with reports of heart attacks, strokes, and exhaustion taking the lives of several dancers.

o Authorities, at a loss to explain or stop the dancing, responded by hiring musicians and building stages, thinking the dancers would eventually tire themselves out.

o This plan backfired, as it seemed to encourage more people to join in. The music and stages turned the crisis into a bizarre city-wide dance marathon.

- The actual cause of the Dancing Plague of 1518 remains a mystery, with theories ranging from mass psychogenic illness to consumption of ergot fungi (which can have effects similar to LSD when ingested).

- One of the more modern theories is that the dancing plague was a result of stress-induced psychosis. This theory takes into account that the region where the victims lived was riddled with starvation and disease, and the inhabitants were superstitious and prone to magical thinking.

- The dancing epidemic did not stop until September when the dancers were whisked away to a mountaintop shrine to pray for absolution.

- In a bizarre twist, some sources claim that red shoes were seen as a symbol of the dancing plague, and their usage was subsequently banned in some regions of Europe.

- The Dancing Plague of 1518 is not the only recorded incident of its kind. There have been similar outbreaks in Switzerland, Germany, and Holland, though none as large as the one in Strasbourg.

- This event has been used in literature and art as a metaphor for mindless adherence to a destructive course of action.

- Though the event is often called "The Dancing Plague," the term "dance" is a misnomer. Eyewitness accounts describe participants as being in a state of unconsciousness, and their movements were more akin to convulsions.

- Despite its name and fame, the Dancing Plague is not a recognized medical condition today.

- Some accounts suggest that those who were afflicted felt as though they were being danced by some invisible force, that they were not in control of their own bodies.

- The 2008 book "The Dancing Plague: The Strange, True Story of an Extraordinary Illness" by John Waller provides a detailed account of this mysterious event.

- This strange event has been the subject of numerous studies, with modern medical scholars trying to find a plausible explanation for the sudden and widespread dancing frenzy.

- Despite all the theories, no definitive explanation for the dancing plague has ever been agreed upon.

- Today, the Dancing Plague of 1518 is remembered as one of history's strangest events, where an outbreak of dancing brought a city to a standstill, and caused death and disorder on a mass scale.

Chapter 57
The Curse of the Hope Diamond
The Deaths and Misfortunes Surrounding This Infamous Jewel

- The Hope Diamond is one of the most famous jewels in the world, with ownership records dating back four centuries.

- It weighs a staggering 45.52 carats and is notable for its rare blue color and beautifully intricate cut.

- The diamond's origin is believed to be India, where it was purchased in the 17th century by French gem merchant Jean-Baptiste Tavernier.

- The diamond was sold to King Louis XIV of France, where it became known as the "Blue Diamond of the Crown" or "French Blue." During the French Revolution, it was stolen and disappeared for a couple of decades.

- In 1839, the diamond reemerged in the gem collection catalog of Henry Philip Hope, which is where it gets its current name.

- The Hope Diamond is infamous for the curse it supposedly puts on those who own or wear it. The curse is said to bring bad luck and tragedy to the person who possesses the gem.

- Many owners of the Hope Diamond, and their families, have indeed suffered misfortune, bankruptcy, and death, which further perpetuates the curse legend.

- One of the first victims of the alleged curse was Tavernier, who was reportedly torn apart by a pack of wild dogs after he sold the diamond.
- King Louis XVI and Queen Marie Antoinette, who owned the diamond, were beheaded during the French Revolution.
- A later owner, Wilhelm Fals, a Dutch jeweler, was allegedly killed by his son, who then committed suicide.
- Another owner, Greek merchant Simon Montharides, was killed along with his entire family when they were pushed off a precipice in a carriage accident.
- Even newspaper and mail carrier James Todd, who delivered the Hope Diamond to its current home, the Smithsonian Institution, suffered a crushed leg and head injury in accidents, and his house burned down.
- However, skeptics argue that the curse is nothing more than a sensational story perpetuated by journalists and gem dealers to increase the diamond's mystique and value.
- Despite its infamous curse, the Hope Diamond has managed to captivate millions of visitors at the Smithsonian Institution in Washington D.C., where it is currently housed.
- The diamond is set in a pendant and surrounded by 16 white diamonds. The necklace chain contains another 45 white diamonds.
- The Hope Diamond has an intense blue coloration due to trace amounts of boron in the stone.
- Under ultraviolet light, the Hope Diamond emits a red phosphorescent glow. Once the light source is removed, the diamond continues to glow for some time.
- The Hope Diamond is insured for $250 million.
- In 2010, the Hope Diamond was displayed as a stand-alone gem with no setting, the first time in more than two centuries.
- Despite its notorious reputation, the Hope Diamond remains one of the most popular exhibits at the Smithsonian Institution, attracting millions of visitors each year who are eager to catch a glimpse of this legendary gem.

Chapter 58
The Voynich Manuscript
The Book That Has Stumped Scholars for Centuries

- ○ The Voynich Manuscript is a mysterious, hand-written and illustrated codex that has baffled historians, cryptographers, and linguists for over a century.

- ○ The manuscript is named after Wilfrid Voynich, a Polish book dealer who purchased it in 1912.

- ○ The manuscript is currently housed in Yale University's Beinecke Rare Book and Manuscript Library.

- ○ The manuscript is written in an unknown script of which no other example has been found.

- ○ It is written from left to right, and there's a consensus that it appears to be a real language—just one that nobody has been able to decode.

- ○ The Voynich Manuscript contains approximately 240 pages, some of which fold out, and is illustrated with botanical, anatomical, and astronomical drawings.

- ○ The illustrations suggest it might be a scientific or medical text, dealing with matters of herbal medicine, astronomy, and the zodiac, but that's merely speculative.

- Carbon dating places the creation of the manuscript to the early 15th century (1404-1438).

- Many of the plants illustrated in the botanical section do not resemble any known species, adding another layer of mystery.

- Cryptographers and codebreakers from both World Wars I and II have studied the manuscript, but none have successfully cracked the code.

- Some theories suggest that the manuscript may have been a pharmacopoeia, a book containing instructions on how to make medicinal drugs.

- The manuscript's text has resisted all attempts at translation, leading some to label it a hoax.

- One of the most popular theories is that the manuscript is a case of steganography, where the meaningful information is hidden within irrelevant information.

- Theories about the manuscript's origins are abundant and include associations with famous historical figures like Leonardo da Vinci and Roger Bacon.

- In 2004, a team of experts at the University of Arizona performed radiocarbon dating on the manuscript's vellum, affirming that it dated from the early 15th century.

- The ink on the manuscript was analyzed and found to be made of iron gall ink, which was commonly used during the Middle Ages.

- In 2014, Stephen Bax, a linguistics professor, claimed he had deciphered 14 characters and 10 words in the manuscript, but this claim has been disputed.

- Some pages of the manuscript are missing, with the existing text showing signs of having been rewritten.

- The manuscript has been the subject of numerous books, documentaries, and even inspired elements in popular culture, including novels and video games.

- Despite a myriad of attempts to crack its code, the Voich Manuscript remains one of the most enigmatic documents in the world, continuing to draw the fascination of scholars, cryptographers, and those intrigued by unexplained mysteries.

Chapter 59
The Brown Mountain Lights
The Glowing Orbs in the North Carolina Mountains

- The Brown Mountain Lights are a series of ghost lights reported near Brown Mountain in North Carolina.

- These lights have been seen for hundreds of years and are one of North Carolina's most famous enduring mysteries.

- The lights are usually red, blue, green, or white and are described as resembling a lantern or ball of fire.

- Witnesses often report seeing the lights floating over the mountain, and occasionally moving in erratic patterns.

- There's no definitive explanation for the phenomenon, although theories range from extraterrestrial life to ghosts.

- The Brown Mountain Lights have become part of local folklore, inspiring countless ghost stories and local legends.

- The best times to view the lights are reportedly September and October, although sightings have occurred throughout the year.

- One legend claims the lights are the spirits of Cherokee and Catawba Indians killed in a massive battle on Brown Mountain.

- The lights were first reported in print in 1913, although sightings date back to long before then.

- One popular viewing spot for the lights is the Brown Mountain Overlook off North Carolina Highway 181.

- The United States Geological Survey has attempted to study the lights on multiple occasions but has never reached a definitive explanation.

- Some researchers speculate the lights could be a form of natural plasma, similar to ball lightning, caused by geological activity.
- A song about the Brown Mountain Lights was written by Scotty Wiseman in the 1950s and has been covered by many artists since then.
- Despite the many theories, none have been universally accepted, and the Brown Mountain Lights continue to be a topic of debate and fascination.
- There are annual "Brown Mountain Lights" festivals and symposiums, bringing together locals and tourists interested in the phenomenon.
- Many people also believe the lights are related to UFO activity due to their unpredictable movements and appearances.
- Scientific research into the Brown Mountain Lights has included investigation into the piezoelectric effect, which occurs when pressure is applied to certain materials, causing them to emit electricity.
- The phenomenon has been featured on TV shows such as "The X-Files" and "Ancient Aliens", reflecting its ongoing allure.
- Multiple YouTube videos purport to show the lights, though skeptics often dismiss these as hoaxes or misinterpretations of more mundane phenomena.
- Despite scientific skepticism and lack of definitive explanation, the Brown Mountain Lights continue to captivate the public imagination as an unexplained and elusive mystery.

Conclusion

Congratulations! You've journeyed through the fascinating realm of monsters, and I hope it has sparked as much joy and curiosity for you as it does for me. It's been a thrill sharing these captivating tidbits, and I hope they'll provide you with intriguing conversation starters and a fresh appreciation for the bizarre and unexplained.

But the quest for knowledge doesn't stop here! If you're ready for more thrilling trivia and remarkable revelations, there's great news for you. 'The Monster Guide' is just the first installment of the 'Interesting Facts For Interesting People' series. Coming up next are 'The Science Guide', 'The Nature Guide', and 'The Space Guide', each brimming with absorbing facts and insights. So stay tuned, and thank you for embarking on this fantastic journey with me. Here's to discovering more together in the next book!

Made in the USA
Coppell, TX
23 July 2023

19511057R00090